MW01254414

freedom,
the spirit
triumphant

Translated from the French
Original title: LA LIBERTÉ, VICTOIRE
DE L'ESPRIT

Omraam Mikhaël Aïvanhov

Freedom, the Spirit Triumphant

2nd edition
Second printing March 2000

Izvor Collection — No. 211

P R O S V E T A

Canadian Cataloguing in Publication Data

Aïvanhov, Omraam Mikhaël, 1900-1986
    Freedom, the spirit triumphant

    (Izvor collection ; 211)
    Translation of: La liberté, victoire de l'esprit.
    ISBN 1-895978-13-0

    1. Free will and determinism. 2. Liberty. I. Title.
II. Series: Izvor collection (North Hatley, Quebec) ; 211.

BJ1462.A4913 2000   123'.5   C00-900438-6

Prosveta Inc.
3950, Albert Mines, North Hatley, QC, Canada J0B 2C0

        Prosveta S.A. — B.P. 12 — 83601 Fréjus Cedex (France)

TABLE OF CONTENTS

One	Man's Psychic Structure	11
Two	Mind over Matter	31
Three	Fate and Freedom	45
Four	Freedom through Death	65
Five	Sharing in the Freedom of God	71
Six	True Freedom: a Consecration of Self	89
Seven	Freedom through Self-Limitation ..	103
Eight	Anarchy and Freedom	115
Nine	The Notion of Hierarchy	131
Ten	The Synarchy Within	147

1

MAN'S PSYCHIC STRUCTURE

All my life long I have been intent on one thing and one thing only: how to help my fellow human beings. This is my one great concern, my only preoccupation. I am well aware of the conditions in which they live; indeed, I would have to be blind not to recognize all the difficulties they have to face. But it is possible to overcome these difficulties; there are a certain number of methods by means of which men and women can strengthen their inner life and, if they are to avoid being destroyed by external conditions, they must learn to use them.

The table that you see here (Figure 1) sums up in a few key words all the methods contained in our Teaching and I imagine that you have never seen another quite like it. At first sight, it is simply a collection of isolated words with no apparent relation to each other, but once they have been explained to you and linked up, each in its proper place in the whole, their meaning and the realities to which they correspond will become clear to you, for this table presents a synopsis or overall view of human psychic structure and the activities which correspond to each of man's faculties.

As you can see, the table is divided into five columns. The first column shows man's basic structure, the constituent **principles** of a human being: the physical body, the will, heart, intellect, soul and spirit.

The second column indicates the **ideal** towards which each basic principle tends. Each principle, of course, has a different ideal.

In order to attain its ideal, each principle must find strength, support and nourishment, and the third column indicates the type of **nourishment** or food required in each case.

The fourth column indicates the **price** that has to be paid to obtain that food; and the fifth column indicates the **activity** or type of work that has to be done in order to earn the wages to pay that price.

As you can see, all these different notions hang together in a perfectly logical and coherent manner. But I think you will understand the whole thing better if I begin by explaining what concerns the physical body, for that is something visible and tangible, something that is familiar to

PRINCIPLE	IDEAL	NOURISHMENT	PAYMENT	ACTIVITY
SPIRIT	ETERNITY	FREEDOM	TRUTH	IDENTIFICATION UNION
SOUL	THE INFINITE	IMPERSONALITY	ECSTASY	PRAYER ADORATION CONTEMPLATION
INTELLECT	KNOWLEDGE LIGHT UNDERSTANDING	THOUGHT	WISDOM	MEDITATION
HEART	WARMTH HAPPINESS	FEELINGS	LOVE	MUSIC ART HARMONY
WILL	POWER MOVEMENT	STRENGTH	GESTURE BREATH	EXERCICES GYMNASTICS
PHYSICAL BODY	HEALTH LIFE	FOOD	MONEY	WORK

Figure 1.

us all : no one can doubt the reality of the physical body.

The ideal of the physical body is health. Nothing is more precious, more essential to the physical body than to be healthy, vigorous and strong and, of course, this means that the body has to have food in solid, liquid and gaseous form. If it does not get that food it dies. We all need food in order to live : everyone knows that, even children. But to obtain food, we need money and to get money we have to work. You all know the story of Antonio, the labourer who spent his days breaking stones. One day someone asked him, 'Hey, Antonio, what are you breaking stones for?' 'For money!' replied Antonio. 'And what do you want money for?' 'For macaroni!' 'And what do you want macaroni for?' 'To eat, of course!' 'Why do you want to eat?' 'To be strong.' 'And why do you want to be strong?' 'I need to be strong to break stones!' You see : it's a vicious circle! But you all agree, of course: in order to eat we have to have money and in order to earn money we have to work. It is quite simple!

But just a minute: if that seems so simple and obvious on the physical level, have you never thought that the same pattern can be found on the other levels? The will, heart, intellect, soul and spirit of man all tend towards a goal, and in order to attain their respective goals they all need food of some kind; in order to get food they have to have money, and in order to earn money each has to perform some particular type of work. Once you have really grasped all the elements of this table you will possess the key to man's psychic life.

The physical body, obviously, is the foundation on which the other, subtler principles are based. The soul and the spirit, for example, cannot truly be said to be in the body, but they manifest through the body; through the brain, the solar plexus, the eyes and so on. When you look at someone very lovingly, with a look of great purity and light, who is it that is looking out through your eyes? The eyes belong to the physical body, true, but who is it who manifests himself through them, who uses the means of expression they provide? Is it the soul or the spirit? Is it God Himself? And if you shoot a black look full of hatred at someone, or say something so terrible that it makes them ill, it is because hostile forces have used you to harm them. Our physical body, therefore, is often no more than the instrument of forces which exist in it or outside it and which can be either beneficial or malicious.

Now what is the ideal of the will? The will seeks power and movement. Perhaps you will say,

'But the will can also ask for wisdom, intelligence or beauty.' No, the will is not interested in wisdom, intelligence and beauty. These belong to other principles. The will can be recruited in the work of acquiring intelligence or creating a work of art, but the only thing it wants for itself, the only things that really interest it are power and movement. The will hates to be inactive; it needs to be constantly busy, touching things, moving them about, going from one place to another.

But, just as the physical body can do nothing without food, the will cannot attain its ideal without nourishment either, and the nourishment of the will is strength. When it is nourished by strength, the will is dynamic and energetic, but without it, it wilts and wastes away. And the element which serves as money for the will to buy the food it needs, is action, gestures. Yes, it is important to shake oneself free from the grip of immobility and inertia in order to stimulate and set in motion the energies of the will. By learning to bestir itself and take action, the will 'buys' strength and becomes powerful. And the very first movement is the act of breathing. When a newborn child draws its first breath it sets in motion all the other processes of life.

If you want to earn the kind of 'money' that will buy food for the will, you must get into the habit of practising certain exercises such as those which are recommended in our Teaching: the breathing exercises, a few very simple gymnastics[1] and the Paneurythmic dances. All these exercises are designed to strengthen the will. Of course, you will have to add to this all the ordinary activities of everyday life, but there is no need for me to go into details: there are too many of them and, besides, you all know them. The exercises I have mentioned are those which have a particular significance for the spiritual life.

Perhaps you will say that you never thought that these exercises could do much to strengthen your will; that they were only designed to stimulate your physical vitality and, perhaps, to cheer your hearts. Of course, they do that too, because everything is connected. At the moment, for the sake of clarity, I am separating all the different levels so as to see exactly what corresponds to each, but in fact, of course, the different levels cannot be isolated from each other. When you do the breathing exercises or the gymnastics, the body benefits from them also: you enjoy better health, you feel an influx of vigour, good humour and cheerfulness and your ideas are clearer; that is absolutely true. Nothing exists in isolation; everything is connected.

1. See 'Complete Works', volume 13.

And now let's look at the 'heart'. Human beings possess a faculty which enables them to have feelings and emotions: this is what we call the heart. It is not the physical heart known to anatomy and physiology which is a kind of hydraulic pump and the principal organ of the blood system. The true organ of feelings and emotion that I am referring to, and which I have often talked about, is the solar plexus, and we shall certainly come back again to this on some other occasion.[2]

What is the heart's ideal? Does it clamour for knowledge, learning or power? No, the heart seeks happiness, joy and warmth, for it comes to life only in the warmth. Cold is fatal to it. Wherever it goes it seeks the warmth of its fellow-creatures. The heart feeds on feelings: every sort and kind of feeling both good and bad — unfortunately! But as we cannot talk about everything we shall only talk about the positive feelings which fill the hearts of the Sons and Daughters of God.

Happiness and joy have to be paid for with the coin of love. If you love, then immediately your heart is nourished. Haven't I told you this time and time again? Nothing else can give you happiness, neither wealth nor power nor even

2. See, *The Solar Plexus and the Brain* in 'Complete Works', volume 6.

beauty: only love. Love is the only thing that brings happiness. Whatever else you give your heart it will never be satisfied, it will continue to plead for love, because love is the only currency with which it can buy whatever it needs. When you love someone, your love is a coin which enables you to 'buy' all kinds of sensations, feelings and emotions. Love gives birth to thousands of different sensations every day. When your love runs out it is your money that has run out, and then you have no more emotions and sensations, you cannot feel anything any more! No matter how much you embrace your wife, if you don't love her any more you will not get any joy or happiness out of it. But if you love her — Oh, joy! Even without touching her you are thrilled by the thousands of wonderful sensations and feelings that race through you. Feelings which are quite impossible to analyse, but you experience them simply because love is there!

The ideal of the intellect is knowledge, and in order to obtain knowledge, the intellect must be given it's own special kind of food, which is thought. Naturally, when we speak of thoughts we also have to include evil thoughts, for just like the heart which can feed on evil feelings, the mind can feed on many different kinds of thoughts; but here too, I only want to talk about the best and most luminous thoughts. Thought is the

food of the mind: if you don't think you will
never know anything. Some people say, 'Why
bother our heads? It's not good to think too
much, you can go mad that way!' Yes, if you
think in the wrong way you can, indeed, go
mad! But to think clearly and correctly is the best
possible way of nourishing the intellect. If you
don't feed your mind it will grow dull and feeble
because you are leaving it to die of hunger.

Here, too, if you want to purchase the best
kind of thoughts with which to feed your mind
you will need money, and that money is wisdom.
Wisdom is the only currency which can be
exchanged for the kind of thoughts which will
enable your intellect to acquire the light it seeks.
Wisdom is money, gold — gold from the sun!
Yes, wisdom is spiritual gold and it comes straight
from the sun. All the heavenly wares stored in
the 'shops' on High can be bought with the
gold coin of wisdom in exactly the same way as
we can buy whatever we want in the shops on
earth with our physical gold. If you go and ask
for what you want from a celestial shop, the entities in charge will ask you if you can pay for it in
gold, and if you can they will give you everything
you ask for, if not you will come away empty-
handed.

In order to obtain this gold, of course, you
have to work: you have to read, study, reflect

and meditate, and although the synoptic table does not mention that you also have to go and contemplate the rising sun, you can add this for yourselves : in spring and summer you must assist at the sunrise so as to receive gold from the sun.

And what about the soul ? What is the soul's ideal ? This will perhaps surprise you, but the soul does not aspire to knowledge, light or happiness. The ideal pursued by the soul is space, immensity. It asks only to be allowed to expand, to stretch, to reach out and embrace the infinite. The soul longs for the infinite ; it suffers when it feels hemmed in. The human soul is a part of the Universal Soul and in the prison of our bodies it feels stifled and constricted and longs to expand freely. Most people imagine that a man's soul is wholly contained within him, but that is not so : in fact only a small portion of our soul dwells within us, all the rest leads its own independent life outside us, floating in the Cosmic Ocean. But when the Universal Soul has some special plan for us, when It wants to animate and vivify us and make us more beautiful, It seeks to enter into us and impregnate every part of our being more fully. So our soul is not limited to our own little persons, it is something immensely greater and it is constantly reaching for immensity and infinite space.

But in order to attain its goal the soul, too, needs to keep up its strength, and it can only do this if it has the right food. The soul feeds on the qualities and virtues of our higher conscious-ness: impersonality, abnegation and sacrifice; all those things which enable man to free himself from his own limits and conquer his self-centredness. As soon as someone says, 'That's mine !' he has put up a barrier and created a sepa-ration, whereas an impersonal attitude breaks down and removes barriers.

The soul, too, must have money in order to purchase food, and the only coin capable of buy-ing the food that will enable the soul to attain its goal of infinity is ecstasy, the state in which our beings expand and fuse into one with the divine Being; and the activity which enables us to reach that sublime state is prayer: prayer, adoration and contemplation. To pray is to search for divine Splendour, and when man succeeds in making contact with that Splendour, his whole being expands and he feels as though he were being torn from his own body. This is ecstasy. All those who have ever experienced it tell us that they were no longer confined within the limits of their bodies on earth; they felt themselves to be immersed in the Universal Soul, melted and welded into one with It.

The soul is the pre-eminent expression of the feminine principle, its most marvellous, divine expression. The spirit, on the other hand, is the divine expression of the masculine principle. The intellect and heart also represent the two principles, but on a lower level. This alternate manifestation of the two principles is a pattern which repeats itself throughout all the regions and levels of the universe in different forms : positive and negative, emissive and receptive, and so on ; the masculine and feminine principles are present everywhere.

What does the spirit ask for ? Not space or knowledge, not happiness or power or health. No, it needs none of those things because it is never ill or weak or unhappy, never lost in the dark or the cold. The spirit asks for one thing and one thing only : eternity. The essence of the spirit is immortal and it refuses to be bound by time : its goal is eternity, and just as the dimension in which the soul is at home is space, so the dimension of the spirit is time. This is what makes me say to physicists and philosophers that they will never grasp the true nature of space and time until they understand the nature of the soul and spirit. Space and time are notions which belong to a fourth dimension, and the soul and spirit are in touch with this dimension. Men of science will

never plumb the mysteries of space and time
until, in their own souls and spirits, they have
consciously sought to penetrate the mysteries of
infinity and eternity.

In order to attain eternity — or rather, in
order to introduce eternity into our human consciousness, for the spirit, by its very nature, is
already eternal — the spirit needs its own kind of
food. (Are you surprised when I say that the
spirit, too, needs food? Don't you remember that
I have already told you that even God takes
nourishment?) The food of the spirit is freedom.
The soul needs to spread its wings and free itself
from the restrictions of space, and the spirit needs
to cut all the ties that bind it to time.

But freedom has to be bought and the money
with which the spirit buys freedom is truth.
Neither wisdom nor love are capable of setting
the spirit free: only truth. Every little truth that
you manage to collect about anything at all, frees
you from certain bonds. Jesus told his disciples,
'You will know the truth and the truth will
set you free.' Yes, it is truth which sets us free.
And what about love? Ah, love does just the
opposite; love binds you! Do you want to bind
yourself to something or someone? If so, call
on love: nothing creates a bond stronger than
that created by love. And if you want to set
yourself free, call on truth. If you want proof of

this just look what happens to the old : they begin to know the truth and, since truth is always accompanied by freedom, they begin to free themselves from this world and move on into the next ! Whereas when people are in love they are not interested in freeing themselves, they want to stay on earth together, billing and cooing for ever ! Think about this and you will have to admit that I'm right !

But before we can possess the truth there is work to be done, and that work is to identify ourselves with our Creator. Through the work of identification with God we come closer and closer until we melt into and become one with Him, and in Him is truth. When Jesus said, 'My Father and I are one,' he was expressing this work of identification, and we have to do this same work in order to earn the gold we call truth. And that truth is that man is a spirit, a spark from the divine fire that is God, and that he will one day return to God. This, then, is the truth! Once man has truly seen, understood and felt this reality within himself, he is free : free from his own passions and worldly ambitions, free from pain and anguish. He has taken the first step into eternity.

The fact that I associate freedom with the dimension of time rather than that of space will, perhaps surprise many of you. 'Surely', they will say; 'To be free is to be able to move about, not to be hampered in one's movements. Doesn't this mean that freedom belongs to the soul rather than to the spirit?' No, you must not confuse freedom with space. True freedom is not a question of being able to move about as one pleases. Picture a man who is so fed up with his mother-in-law that he packs his bags and goes off to the top of a mountain to escape from her. But he soon finds that he has not really freed himself from her. Why? Because his mind is still rehashing all the same old arguments, the same old resentments. He may be far away from her, physically, but mentally she is still with him, because he can't stop thinking about her — and what lovely, luminous thoughts they are too! The notion of liberty, freedom, is not tied to that of space because no amount of space can give you true freedom. It can give a certain form of freedom: if you have space you can move freely and go from one place to another, but true freedom is something quite different. True freedom is the consciousness of eternity.

Jesus said, 'And this is eternal life, that they may know You, the only true God.' What kind of 'knowing' was Jesus talking about? Certainly something other than the intellectual knowledge of someone who has read a few books and says,

'I know all about it!' True knowledge is something quite different: 'To know You, the only true God' implies union with God, identification with Him, and man can only identify and melt into oneness with God through his spirit: only when he has achieved this will man be truly free.

Are you beginning to get a sense of the truth of what I have been saying? Obviously, if you listen to me with a purely objective, intellectual attitude you may not feel anything at all. In fact the only effect will be to leave you with the conviction that what I say contradicts your own opinions. Well, it is not my fault if contemporary culture has put so many ideas into your heads which prevent you from understanding me. But hurry up and adopt my point of view and you will see: you will be filled with wonder! I can hear you saying, 'Yes, now I understand how important the table is. I'm going to keep it on me so that I can take it out and look at it wherever I go, in the train or on the bus, at the dentist's and even at the hairdresser's — why not?' Yes, the synoptic table can help you enormously; never underestimate its importance.

2

MIND OVER MATTER

Man possesses a spirit which is divine in its essence and which participates in all that exists in the universe. He also possesses physical organs which are designed to communicate with the spirit, but as the matter of these organs is not very subtle nor highly refined, very few of the messages transmitted by his spirit ever reach his consciousness. This is why, just as the alchemists of old concentrated on trying to transform and transmute matter, modern man must concentrate his efforts on his physical body in order to make it pure, spiritual and divine.

The alchemists were right to concentrate on matter and to try to transform it, and we must work in the same direction, by giving our physical body pure food and drink, pure air to breathe, the pure rays of the sun and even — perhaps this will surprise you — by surrounding it with all the most beautiful forms, colours and perfumes. The spirit, on the other hand, does not need you to take care of it : it is omniscient, all-powerful and free like God. It is only the material component of your being that needs your attention in order to be transformed and, in this way, provide your spirit with more and better possibilities for manifesting itself on the physical plane.

But this question is still not very clear to many people, even to spiritual people. Many of them, in fact, believe that it is the spirit which needs to be purified and uplifted and that the body can be neglected and even despised. They see that the spirit manifests itself very imperfectly through the medium of the body and so they think that it is the spirit which is imperfect and needs to be developed, strengthened and purified. No, the spirit is a pure spark from God, endowed with an infinite range of faculties, but we must give it the favourable conditions it needs in order to manifest itself properly. There have been cases of people ; thinkers, artists or mystics, who have known such extraordinary states of inspiration and illumination that they have almost physically touched sublime, celestial realities and yet, when they return to their normal state they understand hardly anything about their experience. This makes it very obvious that if man were to improve his powers of receptivity and perception, if he were able to give the spirit the right conditions in order to manifest itself more fully, he would understand what extraordinary things he is capable of.

Take the case of someone who is mentally retarded or physically ill: it is not his spirit that is ill or retarded, the problem lies in the organ by means of which the spirit should be able to manifest itself; the brain. The spirit is in the position of the concert artist who has been given an out-of-tune piano to play on! However hard he tries and however willing and skillful he may be, he will never get anything but discordant noises out of his instrument. You cannot blame the pianist: the fault lies with the piano. The brain which serves as the medium or instrument by means of which the spirit is expected to manifest itself is like the musician's piano. So, you see, man needs to purify the matter of his different bodies (physical, astral and mental), otherwise the spirit will never be able to communicate any of its powers to him. The spirit of man is a divine spark, the power and the omniscience of God are contained in its essence; all it needs is a suitable instrument. And that is what the physical body is: one of the instruments that God has given to man, and it is an instrument fashioned with unutterable wisdom and endowed with a great wealth of resources. And yet some people despise and reject the physical body because it is material whereas the spirit, you understand — well, that is something noble and divine!

Of course, I know you will tell me that that is no longer the case, that people have understood the importance of the physical body. Yes, but the only trouble is that they have not understood it correctly: all they are concerned with is providing the physical body with food and hygiene, comfort and the pleasures of the senses so as to make it attractive and seductive, not so that it will be an instrument of the spirit. The Bible says, 'Do you not know that your body is the temple of the living God?' So it is the body, not the spirit, which is the temple of God. The spirit cannot be a temple because it is immaterial: the spirit is the celebrant, the one who presides over the ceremonies, and the temple is the physical body. It is perfectly clear but this has still not been properly understood. And there are a great many other things in the Gospels which still need to be explained!

The spirit is a son of God, an immortal principle: how could we ever hope to improve or add to it? But the physical body is quite a different proposition: that is where our work lies. Our task is to make it so pure and invulnerable, so unassailable by sickness and disease, so alive and so subtle that it can really and truly become the mouthpiece of the spirit, a means of expression for Heaven itself, so that all the marvels of the universe may be made manifest through it. For the moment, of course, man's physical body is not a temple, it is a tavern, and those who come and carouse in it come from Hell. It is used for all the most abominable purposes ; people think that that is what it is for. Certainly not ! The body has been created to become the ideal instrument of the spirit, and when it does become that perfect instrument it will be capable of healing the sick, of radiating light, of moving freely in space. You will see : one day man will do wonders with his physical body. It is very easy for the spirit : as soon as it leaves the heavy, cumbersome body it is free to go wherever it wants, there is nothing to restrict it, it can travel to the depths of the oceans or to the farthest star. But the body is not yet ready to undertake such adventures.

What I have just been saying is extremely important. We can see from the history of mankind that human beings have rarely been capable of assigning the proper place to the spirit and the body. For some, the spirit is the only thing that matters and they despise the body to such an extent that they leave it to die. But if the body were really so despicable, if the spirit were the only thing that mattered, we would have done better never to have come down to earth. We should have stayed up there, in the home of the spirit! But since we came and incarnated on earth we must conclude that it is because there is a great deal of work to be done down here. The role of the spirit is to come down and assume a physical body so as to be able to work on the earth and turn it into a magnificent garden in which the Lord can come and stroll. If man were meant to despise and reject matter why did he ever descend into matter? Why submerge oneself in matter unless it is in order to sublimate it and make it luminous and transparent like the spirit? When Jesus said, 'Thy will be done on earth as it is in Heaven' he was asking this very thing: that the glory of the spirit descend into matter. Unfortunately, when human beings incarnate on earth, they forget the mission that has been assigned to them, so that when they leave the earth again they have done nothing but plunder and defile the matter on which they were supposed to have been working.

The time has come, now, for man to concern himself with matter — and this means our physical bodies, too, as well as the earth itself — to concern himself with it and to transform it by bringing the spirit down into it, for only the spirit can give life, freedom and light. God has endowed man with all the talents and all the powers he needs, but if he does nothing to bring the spirit down into his physical body he is like a barren, uncultivated soil, incapable of producing anything. Although he has everything, potentially, it is as though he had nothing. Ignorance on this score is extremely prejudicial to many people because they see themselves lacking many of the powers and possibilities that others possess and so they believe that they really are poor and deprived whereas others are privileged. No, not at all : they have all the same talents and qualities as the others. It is just that they have not yet managed to manifest them because they have not worked to put their body in tune with their spirit.

The difference which does exist between human beings does not mean that their spirits have reached different levels of evolution. No, all human spirits are sparks of the divine fire, all are a quintessence, a part of God, just as drops of water are miniature replicas of the ocean. All spirits are identical, but as they became separated from God each one had its own particular mission to pursue and each one had to travel through different regions and, in so doing, received different impressions, learned different things and experienced different emotions. The only difference, therefore, lies in the varied experiences they have undergone in different regions. But in their essence, in their quintessence, their sublime nature, they are all identical. Whereas physical bodies are not identical; although they are all built on the model of one perfect prototype, they have all reached different degrees of evolution because their owners have not all worked to the same extent in previous incarnations to make their body a docile instrument of their spirit.

The truth of the matter, therefore, is that we have everything within us. It takes time to materialize, to give concrete form to the possibilities inherent in the spirit: that is certainly true, but our spirit already possesses all the powers and possibilities it needs. If you thought about this truth more often it would be an enormous help to you in your evolution.

Let me give you an example. Human beings have got into the habit of expecting everything they need to come from outside them. On the one hand this is perfectly normal, for they could not survive without many of the things they receive from outside themselves: water, air, the sun and food, for instance. We are creatures, and all creatures, the whole of creation is obliged to get something, if only its food, from outside itself. Only the Creator can escape from this law, He does not need others to provide food for Him. Yes, but as He has placed something of Himself in every one of His creatures — that spark of God, that spirit which partakes of the divine nature — every creature can call on that spirit to create whatever it needs. Instead of always looking for help from outside, therefore — which can be extremely detrimental, for often enough, the help one waits for does not turn up — human beings can act inwardly by their thoughts, their wills and their spirits and capture the elements they need to heal or nourish themselves. This is why the Teaching I am bringing you is the Teaching of the spirit, of the Creator, not of matter or creation. If you don't accept and adhere to this Teaching of the spirit, of creation, you will remain forever weak, limited and dependent.

The great mistake of human beings has been to identify so completely with matter that they have become rooted, bogged down in matter, and no longer have the strength to react. It never occurs to them that they could and should identify with the spirit, the spirit which needs nothing extraneous in order to create, which draws the elements it needs from within itself, just as the Lord created the earth out of His own quintessence.

But the time has come, now, to free yourselves from the falsehood of matter and enter into the inner reality of the spirit which is the reality of all the great Masters. Think about this: the Creator and the creatures. It is up to you to decide whether you are going to remain a creature or become a creator. Do you believe me when I tell

you this? Perhaps none of you believes me? No,
I know that you do believe me, but you say, 'Oh,
Master — if only I could do as you say! But life is
so difficult. We don't have the conditions we
need? How well I know it! I know it better than
you do. Where do you think I live? In exactly the
same conditions as you, in the same circumstances, the same world. Yes, but I think differently from you: that is the only difference.

So stop looking outside yourselves for help.
And stop believing, also, that all your troubles
come from outside yourselves. Most people
believe that they are blameless: nothing is ever
their fault, it is always their husband or the neighbours or the government that is at fault, unless it
is because they do not have enough money, or
because the food was bad or the weather foul!
They will never admit that it is their hateful
philosophy that gets them into such dire straits,
and yet it is so. It is their false outlook on life that
has plunged them gradually deeper and deeper
into their problems. The philosophy of matter
simply must be replaced by the philosophy of the
spirit, because that is the only way for human
beings to become strong, powerful, independent
and free.

Now, think about this. What is true for creatures is not true for the Creator. Creatures are too
dependent on the outside world, on their circum-

stances: they are pulled first in one direction and then in another, and they are forced to submit. So become creators; enter into the world of the spirit which creates and shapes its own circumstances, and you will find that everything changes: you will no longer be so dependent on the world around you, you will be free and masters of your own destiny.

3

FATE AND FREEDOM

I

Generally speaking, the first beginnings of something are a sure indication of how it will end; however, if man makes a deliberate effort to divert the normal course of events he can sometimes do so. True, there are a certain number of cases in life in which events unfold with implacable inevitability and which we can predict with total accuracy, just as astronomers can predict eclipses and conjunctions or oppositions of planets, because everything unfolds according to strict mathematical laws. But if the spirit decides to intervene and manifest itself, it can accelerate or delay certain aspects of the process. In our present state of evolution, our spirit is unable to manifest itself fully and absolutely, for it is still subject to the limits imposed on it by matter. In its essence and when it is operating in its own higher sphere, its powers are unlimited: it is only in the sphere of matter that it is still hindered from

manifesting the full range of its powers, for it
takes a long time to organize everything. But it is
ceaselessly active, day by day, gradually working
its way through; in the long run, it is the spirit
which will triumph and transform and govern all
things. For the spirit possesses what we call
'supernatural' powers. In fact there is nothing
supernatural about its powers: miracles, prodi-
gies or extraordinary events which seem to us to
fly in the face of the laws of nature are neither
supernatural nor supra-natural nor anti-natural!
It is simply that they are subject to other laws, the
laws of the spirit.

The task of a disciple can be summed up in
very few words: instead of letting his lower,
animal nature get the upper hand and enslave his
spirit, smothering the divine spark and driving
him out of Paradise, he works according to the
rules of Heaven, abiding by the law of the spirit
and calling on the forces and powers of eternity to
help him to bring down into his daily life other
elements, other quintessences which he already
possesses on the most exalted level of his being.
By means of his thoughts and feelings, by means
of his faith and the efforts he exerts, he adds
something to the ordinary development of
events; something vibrant and radiant, something which shows forth the spirit, the shining
glory of the divine world.

The question of destiny — the problem about whether and to what extent man is free or bound to a predetermined fate — has been under discussion for hundreds and hundreds of years. The great mistake is to believe that all human beings without exception are necessarily bound by the same laws. Obviously, if they behave like animals which obey their sensations and passions and their purely instinctive impulses, then they come under the rule of fate: their lives will adhere strictly to the pattern written in the stars. Whereas those who are much more highly evolved, escape the clutches of fate and enter into the world of Providence and Grace in which reign light and liberty. The great Masters of humanity belong to this second category, but most men drift in a middle zone, somewhere between animals and divinities: in some areas they are bound, in others they are free. You must not think that everyone is free, nor that everyone is subject to an implacable fate. No, the truth is that freedom depends on one's level of evolution. It is man's way of thinking, feeling and behaving which determines how far he is from one or other end of the scale between fate and Providence. Until such time as he attains total freedom, therefore, he is still subject to the law of Karma in some areas of his life, whereas in others he is free. There, quite simply and clearly, you have the truth of the matter.

All kinds of different philosophies concerning freedom are in circulation nowadays, and they all set out to persuade men that they are free. Yes, they may well think that they are free just as long as they know nothing of the pattern on which the universe is built or of the cosmic forces which influence them. They imagine that when they have to decide on a course of action, they are free to choose and decide what to do; it never occurs to them that most of the time they are pawns in the hands of forces they know nothing about. The ancient astrologers used to say that the stars influence but do not determine man or, again, that the wise man is above being influenced by the stars. The stars, therefore, do influence human beings in one direction or the other. When a man is very highly evolved he feels their influence, but they cannot force him into anything against his will. However, when men are still very weak it is a different matter: they behave as though the stars drove them on irresistibly, without their even being aware of it.

Let me illustrate this with an example: when a pretty girl is attracted to a boy she does not have to say 'Come with me. Come and kiss me.' Nor does she have to throw herself at his head. She simply smiles and behaves in such a way as to egg him on, and it is he who starts besieging her with his attentions. She does not say or do anything, and yet she manages to attract him and he, being weak, lets himself be influenced. Well, the stars are rather like pretty girls: they arouse something in you — anger or sensuality, for instance — and then they leave you on your own, because they know very well that you will go all the way. Then they say, 'But we didn't force you; you were free to do as you wanted!' Yes, but by then you have gone too far and the damage is done.

Let me give you some examples that show how events in the lives of some people follow their inevitable, implacable course, whereas for other, more highly evolved people, events move onto another level. Let's say that a highly evolved being has a debt to pay: instead of being obliged to pay it on the physical level, he can pay it on the astral or mental level. One way or another, he has to pay, but he is free to choose and decide on what level he will do so. But others, who are still on the lowest rungs of the evolutionary ladder, are not free to choose: they have to pay in whatever way they are told to. Be sure to remember this and, whatever you do, do not imagine that you can ever get out of paying your debts. You may be allowed to pay them in different ways, but you must pay them. The only freedom involved is in the choice of the currency you will use, but no one is free to avoid a karmic debt.

When astrologers tell people, 'On such and such a day you will have an accident. If you want to avoid it, you must do thus and so', they do not realize that they are encouraging them to behave dishonestly. If we could avoid whatever is supposed to happen to us simply because we know about it in advance it would be too easy: we would be able to avoid everything unpleasant. And, to be quite honest, I have never seen an astrologer who has managed to avoid anything at all! When they foresee that some mishap is supposed to befall them, they take all possible precautions to divert it, but it simply catches up with them in some way they had not expected; and if it does not happen on the exact date they thought it would, it happens a day or two earlier or later!

Nowadays, astrologers are in the habit of saying that events always seem to happen later than the date indicated by their forecasts. Yes; that is true: discrepancies are more frequent today. But if they knew the true science of astrology they would be able to determine the exact moment. There is nothing erratic or unreliable in the heavens; everything is absolutely exact. It is simply that the elements or notions used in modern astrology are not the most perfect or the most adequate, for many aspects of this science have been lost. In the old days, astrologers could give invaluable information and advice because their predictions were very accurate: they could foretell exactly at what time and in what place someone would have an accident, and even what part of his body would be affected. But that kind of knowledge has now been lost.

You probably remember the story told in the 'Tales of a Thousand and One Nights': an astrologer told a rich merchant that his only son would die on a certain date. The merchant, naturally, was dreadfully upset and tried to think of some way of saving his son, so he sent his servants to dig an underground refuge where he would be safe, on a desert island. When the refuge was ready, the servants went back to fetch the young man, but what they did not know was that, in the meantime, a ship had been wrecked not far from the island, and a young prince had escaped from the sinking ship and managed to swim to the island, where he now lived as best he could, eating the wild fruits that grew there.

One day the young prince saw a ship anchoring off the shores of the island. A group of servants, carrying food and bundles of all kinds, came ashore with a very handsome youth and an old man. The whole group went straight to a particular spot where they opened a concealed trap-door and disappeared underground. Shortly after, while the prince was still watching, everybody except the beautiful young man came out into the open and went aboard the ship which immediately sailed away. Once it was out of sight, the prince went straight to where he had seen them disappearing and found a large flat stone with a ring set in it. Seizing the ring he pulled open the trap-door and saw a staircase leading down into a large room, most beautifully furnished and decorated. The young man he had seen with the sailors, earlier, was there, all alone and very alarmed at this unexpected intrusion. However, the prince told him of his own plight and calmed his fears so completely that the young man asked him to stay with him and keep him company.

The two got along very well together and time passed agreeably enough. Then, one very hot day, the young man, who was reclining on his couch, thought he would like a slice of watermelon to quench his thirst, and asked the prince to hand him a knife which was on a shelf over his head. Disaster followed when the prince got his foot tangled in the bed-clothes, lost his balance, and fell on the young man, plunging the knife into his heart and killing him instantaneously. Wild with grief and despair the prince rushed out of the underground chamber and, at that very moment, the merchant's ship came in sight: he was coming to fetch his son, trusting in the prediction that if nothing terrible had happened to him by then (and, of course, he firmly believed that this was the case), he would no longer be in danger. And behold, he found his son lying dead! Now, of course, this is an imaginary tale, but it illustrates the conception that the Ancients had of destiny.

And I have my own ideas on the subject, too. You cannot escape events: what is written is bound to come to pass. I have already told you: the only freedom that a reasonable man enjoys is that of being allowed to pay in different ways. Suppose, for instance, that you know you are going to be seriously ill and that your illness is going to force you to interrupt your work. That illness is a debt you have to pay. Well, you can pay off your debt differently by doing a great deal of spiritual work, with prayer and meditation, so that when the illness strikes it is much less serious than it would have been otherwise and keeps you in bed only a few days: you have paid your debt with light and love. If you live reasonably, spiritually, your whole system will be stronger, and when some mishap occurs because of the aspect or the passage of a certain planet, there will be no lack of 'money' accumulated in your cells with which to pay your debt, that is to say, you will have substantial reserves of strength and energy to help you divert the danger. The reasonable, intelligent, pure life you lead saves up a lot of 'money' in your system and, thanks to your savings, you are in a position to pay your debts quite easily.

Yes, perhaps you find this a bit surprising, but a spiritual Teaching teaches you how to save money — symbolically speaking! Through meditation, prayer and contemplation you can put a handful of gold dust into your bank account on High every day, and when you find yourself in difficulty, instead of trying to cheat and avoid honouring your debts, you can use some of that gold you have saved. This is why I say that you must never again say, 'What's the use of an Initiatic Teaching, and all those spiritual exercises? They don't bring us wealth or fame!' If that is your attitude it only shows how ignorant you are. Spiritual acquisitions are like money: they can be saved up and used when you find yourself in a tight corner.

A few days ago I had a visit from somebody who wanted to talk about her problems. I listened to what she told me, and then I said, 'Judging from what you say, dear lady, your health is good, you have plenty of money and a good education; you have no worries and, above all, you are free to devote all your time to the things you enjoy. But instead of being happy you are constantly depressed and miserable?' 'That's just it', she replied; 'I don't know what the future has in store for me and it worries me dreadfully!' You see? People are always thinking about the future and, as they do not know what it will be like, their imagination runs riot and invents all kinds of disasters. People make themselves unhappy; they never see how rich they really are nor how many possibilities are open to them, how much freedom they have. None of that means anything to them: freedom bores them; instead of using it intelligently they spend all their free time worrying about the future!

The trouble is that human beings are not sufficiently convinced that the kind of future they will have is determined by the way they are living here and now, in the present. Their present is the 'stuff' of which their future will be built. And this means that it is *now* that counts. The future is simply an extension of the present and the present is nothing more than a consequence of the past. Everything is linked together: past, present and future cannot be separated. Your future will be built on the foundations you are laying for it today. If the foundations are not sound, of course, you cannot expect the future to be anything special, and if they are good, then there is no need to worry about the future. The trunk, the branches and the fruit of your tree will be what its roots are. The past is past, but it gave birth to the present, and the present is the roots of the future. It is up to you, to use your spiritual work to build your own future, for that is where your freedom lies: in the construction of your future.

The desperate situation in which mankind finds itself at present, is due to the fact that it has abandoned the great truths of the spirit. This is why a disciple must give priority to the spirit in all his activities: he must proclaim once again the supremacy of the spirit. He must put the seal of the spirit on everything he does, wherever he goes. This is the only way to ensure that he himself and all around him will truly be transformed.

II

When it comes to events of global importance, if Heaven has ordained, for instance, that some grave crisis must strike a particular country, it is only in very rare instances that this can be avoided. But where individuals are concerned, the inevitability of a calamity is not so absolute; an individual has more possibilities open to him to avoid a predicted evil than a state, for instance. Let's say that a war can be foreseen, but there is no way of predicting with absolute certainty that a particular individual will necessarily be killed in that war. The war will take place, as predicted, and there will, obviously, be many dead, but no one can say in advance exactly who will die. An individual always has a slight possibility of escaping a particular destiny.

Let me give you an example of this. Thousands of years before Jesus was born, it had been decreed that he would be betrayed by one of his disciples, but the name of the traitor was never mentioned. Nobody was designated to fill that role until Judas came forward. If he had not been ready to assume the role of traitor, someone else would have done so. The distribution of the different characters in a play is a good illustration of this: you cannot change the characters in a play written by Shakespeare or Molière; there will always have to be a Falstaff or a Harpagon, but the actors who will play these parts are not designated in advance. Those who are best suited to the different roles are chosen when the time comes to complete the cast.

Even Nostradamus did not indicate the persons involved when he made his prophecies. You will probably say, 'But he named names ...more or less explicitly.' Yes, he named names but the identity of the entities who were to assume these names were not revealed in advance. The roles and, sometimes, the names are determined in advance, but not the persons. It is not possible to take someone — Judas, for instance — and keep him bottled up until he is needed, 500 or 2,000 years later, to play the part of traitor! That is not the way things happen, for human beings are free to evolve. It was foreseen, for instance, that Julius Caesar would be murdered, but the murderer was not designated in advance nor, for that matter, was the one who would play the part of Caesar.

The beings who eventually filled these roles had gradually become suited to them during the course of their evolution.

The Lord has never obliged any of His creatures to play a predetermined part, for that would mean that He allowed them no freedom. Human beings are free to develop in one or other direction: they are free to advance and free to regress; they are free to become monsters and tyrants or sages and Initiates.

The process of human evolution can be compared to a play written by God. The Lord has a plan for the evolution of humanity, and in order to bring this plan to fruition, all kinds of events have to take place. Actors are needed to fill the key roles in these events, but the Playwright does not decide in advance who is to fill the different roles. Palaces and prisons both exist and it is up to you to decide which you will choose to live in.

So the Lord has written a play which takes billions of years to be acted out. Innumerable actors move on and off stage; they make war, they make peace, they build and they destroy, and it is true that some of the roles have been determined thousands and thousands of years ago, but humanity has not yet got to the epilogue. Sometimes the same actors come on stage again and again, and at other times new ones come on. Yes, the life of the cosmos is a play written by God and it is He, too, who has created the actors, but He has created them with the freedom to choose which parts they want to play.

As I said, no one particular person was designated in advance to fill the role of Judas. It was planned that there would be a Judas to betray Jesus (and there must certainly have been a good many in the world of traitors who were getting ready to act the part), but the person who was eventually attracted to it was the one who had the greatest natural affinity for the role. If God had determined the destiny of all His creatures there would be no such thing as freedom and, consequently, there would be no such thing as responsibility either. What responsibility can a machine, a robot, have? And if man were not responsible for what he did, what possible meaning could life have?

Mankind, the solar system and even the whole cosmos are destined to experience many vicissitudes and they have all been planned in advance. Nothing can change that, the programme has been pre-arranged; but one element in this programme has not been decided in advance, and that is the part that each one of us will play in the whole.

Let me illustrate this with yet another example. Suppose you are travelling on board ship: the ship follows the prescribed travel plan, stopping at various ports on its way, and there is nothing you can do to change that. Nor can you leave the ship, otherwise you would drown. But while you are on it you can spend your time as you please: you can read or talk to a pretty girl or go to sleep in your cabin. You can go up on deck to look at the ocean, you can fish for cod or for whales — the possibilities are endless! So, you see, we are all in the same boat and the route has been marked out by the Lord Himself and no one has the power to change the slightest detail, otherwise all the Lord's plans would come to nothing.

You can do whatever you please with yourself; you can destroy yourself or you can continually improve yourself, but you cannot change the route followed by this ship, the planet earth, as it sails through the cosmic ocean. That old doctrine which the Church taught in the past, that some people were predestined to be damned for all eternity, while others were predestined to be saved, is just not true. It is completely idiotic to believe such a thing! The truth is that human beings decide for themselves whether they are going to be saved or damned by the lives they lead.

4

FREEDOM THROUGH DEATH

Human existence is a struggle between spirit and matter in which, all too often, men attach far more importance to matter than to the spirit. This tendency can be seen most clearly in people's attitude towards death, particularly in the West.

Westerners do everything in their power to avoid death; in fact they consider people who accept death easily to be under-developed or barely civilized. Yes, Western culture and education encourage people to find every possible means to combat death and they cannot understand why Orientals are so serene in the face of it. For them, this tranquil acceptance of death is the mark of the primitive, uncivilized man. But does civilization necessarily mean that one has to keep people alive in spite of dreadful pain and suffering, instead of letting them die in peace? Why not accept the idea of death more readily? Why try to cling to life at all costs?

Death is there in order to solve a great many problems. A lot of people have noticed this but,

unfortunately, not always in the right way. When
a man is up to his eyes in debt he can take the way
out offered by suicide and his creditors are powerless to do anything about it. If he frees himself by
going to another world they cannot sue him any
more, they are obliged to leave him alone. Unfortunately, problems cannot really be solved so easily. If you have not settled a certain number of
questions before leaving this world you will be
pursued by them in the next. Death is not necessarily a solution; it is a genuine liberation only
when one has finished one's business and solved
all one's earthly problems.

Generally speaking, people cling to life on
earth because they do not know that there is
another, better kind of life, and they are ready to
commit every kind of crime to ensure their sur-
vival. In this way they pile up debts and some day
they are going to have to honour them. A
genuinely spiritual man looks at things quite
differently. He thinks: 'Life on earth is a drudg-
ery. Man is hemmed in and limited, beaten and
tormented, abused in every way. Obviously, there
is a good reason for all this, but one day, when I
have done my job, when I have accomplished the
task for which I incarnated, I'll be free to live in
limitless space.' This attitude corresponds to the
truth, and disciples know it, and this is why, in
spite of the fact that they realize that they would

be much better off on the other side, they are not in a desperate hurry to leave. As long as they have still not settled all their problems and finished the work which Heaven has assigned to them, they are not too concerned about all the rest. Their minds are not obsessed with death or anything else except finishing their work. But once their work is done they have no desire to stay on; they know very well that it is not worth clinging to earth.

When an ordinary human being comes to earth he is only interested in taking advantage of everything: he eats and drinks and pursues pleasure, or he uses tooth and nail to carve out a place for himself in the world. But a disciple of an Initiatic Teaching is only interested in doing the work for which Heaven sent him. He does not bother about finding the means to prolong his life on earth; he knows that if he did that he would be depriving himself of the freedom that would be his in the next world. Consider the human body: even though it can be harmonized and purified to the point of vibrating divinely, it will never be other than matter taken from the earth and, as such, it imposes limitations on man.

Repeat to yourselves, every single day: 'I must do my work. It is my spiritual, divine work that is important. That is the only thing worth doing.' If you say this to yourself frequently you will begin to feel free of all the agitation and distress around you; you will become a channel for blessed, beneficial currents and friendly, beneficial entities, and you will begin to understand the meaning of life. As soon as you manage to change your level of consciousness, certain dark, troubling elements will begin to go out from you because you will no longer be satisfying their demands for food and shelter. You will even lose your fear of death.

Death has often been depicted in fearsome forms and colours but, in reality, none of that is true. Death is a liberation. For an Initiate, above all, it is a liberation, for when an Initiate dies he is not simply changing his place of residence, he is going to a royal welcome, he is going to his coronation.

From now on, therefore, you must get this question of death in proper perspective: you must not be afraid of dying. The only thing you should be afraid of is of being prevented from finishing your work. If you have that attitude it changes everything and you have a perfect right to implore Heaven to give you the proper conditions and the time and opportunities you need to finish your work properly. If you pray for your life to be prolonged simply because you want to go on enjoying money and pleasure, well that proves that you have not understood the true meaning of life.

5

SHARING IN THE FREEDOM OF GOD

In the Emerald Tablet we can read these words: 'You shall separate the subtle from the gross with great diligence.' Where, you may wonder, are you to find the subtle and the gross that have to be separated from each other? Are they to be found only in the alchemist's crucible? Or are they to be found in our own inner lives, in our thoughts and feelings? It is Saint Michael, one of the four great Archangels, who has the task of separating things. This is why his feast day falls towards the end of September, because it is he who governs the autumn, the season of separations, when the fruit falls from the tree and the peel from the fruit. Separation, which is an extremely important phase in alchemical work, can be found in every single area of life and, according to the form it takes, we call it cleaning, sorting, decantation, purification and, also, liberation.

Everywhere in life you will find circumstances in which a separation has to be effected.

When a child comes into the world it has to be separated from its mother; you see someone in danger of drowning in the river: he has to be separated from the water; two men have come to blows: if they are not separated they will kill each other. But then it sometimes happens, too, that you may want to separate a boy and girl who are in love, and if you try to do so the result will be just the opposite: they will cling to each other even more closely. Then again, one sometimes tries to bring people together only to find that one's efforts have driven them even further apart.

If you were clairvoyant you would see that human beings are all connected to other creatures, other regions, other entities or occupations by thousands of threads. Everywhere, all around us, there are threads that bind us, but so subtle, so fine, that we cannot see them. But they are there, these etheric threads, and it is important for you to learn to cut some of them, otherwise you will be so hamstrung that you will be unable to move and you will no longer be free.

Ah, but there is a problem here, and that is that you cannot separate yourself from someone or cut the bonds that bind you to something, unless you create new bonds and bind yourself to something or someone else. You cannot be absolutely detached from everything and everyone: there is no such thing as absolute detachment.

Whatever you do, in one way or another, you will always be 'bound'. Suppose that you are tormented by a passion or by a person and you want to free yourself: if you do not know how to set about it your efforts will be doomed to failure. And the way to set about it is not to try and free yourself independently, using only your own resources, but to attach yourself to a different activity or person who is the exact opposite of the one who first captured your loyalty, and bring them face to face with each other. You all know how to do that in everyday life: you use water to put out a fire, you use soap to remove dirt, and so on. You must always take care to find an ally, another force which can help you to overcome whatever torment has you in its grip.

The rule is that you must always try to ally yourself with the opposite of the person or thing you want to free yourself from. Absolute freedom does not exist because the force of attraction is present everywhere. If you want to free yourself from darkness, you have to work with light, because only light has just the right chemical or physical properties needed to dispel the shades of darkness, and once you have bound yourself to light you will be a prisoner in its gravitational field and no longer able to get away from it. But that need not worry you: it is a highly desirable state of affairs to be enslaved to light! That was

what Jesus was talking about when he said,
'Come to me... for my yoke is easy'. Nothing is
better than to be bound hand and foot, utterly
dependent on the divine forces of light. As you
have no hope of freeing yourself from the grip of
the Devil by your own powers, therefore, you have
to put yourself in the hands of the Lord, because
He alone has the power to set you free. Yes, but
you are not completely free even then! Well, so
much the better, because that is true freedom:
you are free when you are God's servant, utterly
dependent on Him and on His wisdom, beauty,
love and eternity. Look at the Angels, they have
no self-will; they are instruments in the hand of
the Lord, they never do anything against His will
and as soon as they receive an order from Him,
they carry it out, in a flash. And yet would you say
that Angels are not free?

I often hear comments from people who,
having no inkling of the true science, and knowing nothing about the nature of man and how he
is built, declare that they don't need God, nor a
Master, nor the light, and that all that should be
done away with! What they do not realize, of
course, is that in putting an end to 'all that' they
will simply be opening the door to other
things. Yes, for, as I have said, nothing and
nobody in the whole universe is completely and
absolutely free and independent. If an object

escapes from the gravitational field of the earth it is instantly drawn into that of the sun. There is no corner of the universe where you can be totally free. You will always be subject to different influences: you may escape from some but you will not be able to avoid falling subject to others. If you refuse to accept positive, beneficial influences, you will inevitably be subject to negative, harmful ones and vice versa. But one thing is certain: you cannot withdraw from all influence. This is why I repeat so often that it is far better to be subject to the Lord's influence, otherwise you will become a victim to that of the Devil.

Now, let me go back for a moment to the words of Jesus that I quoted a few minutes ago: 'Take my yoke upon you... for my yoke is easy and my burden light.' There is a point here that I would like to make clear to you, and that is that good, wisdom, light, kindness — all these things weigh something. True! Their weight is exceedingly light and so highly desirable! But even the sun's rays weigh something. Every form of matter, however subtle, weighs something. Yes, even primeval matter, that which is closest to God Himself, has a certain weight and exerts a certain amount of pressure. So, from this we can conclude that there is no place in the universe in which man could be totally independent, because everywhere in the universe are

forces, influences and entities. Every part of the
universe is 'populated', and when you leave one
zone you necessarily enter another and become
subject to its laws. You might leave one country
in the world because you don't like it or its laws
and customs, but there is no 'No man's land';
you have to go to another country which has
other laws (which may well be worse!), and you
have to get used to them and learn to abide by
them.

Once a reasonable man has understood this
tremendously important truth, he accepts
Christ's yoke, the yoke of light, in order to find
the freedom he desires. If we want to be free we
have to submit to the Divine Will. The freedom
that human beings dream of and which consists
in never having to submit to any authority other
than oneself, simply does not exist. To want that
kind of liberty, that kind of independence, is the
result of ignorance. In that sense it would be true
to say that freedom does not exist any more than
equality. There is no equality in nature. Perhaps
you will object that when men speak of equality
they mean equality before the law. Yes, but even
there, there is no equality, for if you are rich,
influential and well-informed you will be able to
invoke other laws than those which will be
invoked for someone who is poor, ignorant and
without influence.

You must understand that in order to be truly free you have to become the servant of the only Being who is absolutely free, God Himself. Only God is free; no other being in the whole universe is totally free, not even the Seraphim. Only God is absolutely free and dependent on no one. He is sole Master and Lord, and yet He has accepted to impose limitations on Himself by creating. In creating the world He had to submit to certain limitations, and that part of Him which is limited abides by the laws which He Himself laid down. If you aspire to be free, therefore, become servants of God, become one with Him, because then the freedom which is His will pass into you. You can be free only with God's own freedom; there is no other! This is something that even philosophers have never understood. They imagine that they can be free apart from God. No, never! And those who adhere to that pernicious philosophy and mislead people into getting rid of their sense of religion and cutting themselves off from the Creator, are very ignorant; sooner or later they will have to suffer the consequences of that ignorance.

The degree of freedom you enjoy depends entirely on where you stand on the evolutionary ladder. If you are on the lowest rungs there can be no freedom for you. Are animals free? Are plants, stones or insects free? To be free you have to rise as high as God. Only when you reach the top of the ladder can you be free; nowhere else. Only the Lord is free; no creature is free, not even the Archangels. On the contrary, their whole being is completely submerged in the soul of God; they are subject to His influence. You could say that they are free with the freedom of God, but they are not free *from* God. Only God is free, and His creatures share more and more fully in His freedom as they progress towards Him.

Imagine for a moment that you wanted to cut yourself off completely from the world around you and never go out of your house. In view of this you have stored quantities of food in your attic, but your reserves are not unlimited and you will only be able to eat and drink and stay alive as long as you still have some supplies in reserve. And when all your supplies have run out, then what will happen? Well, you will simply die! Those who have cut their ties with Heaven are living on their reserves, and their reserves are not unlimited either. They say, 'We're perfectly fit and well; we can work like anybody else, and business is flourishing!' Perhaps, but one day their supplies will run out and death will be imminent: spiritual death. Human beings are so ignorant that they get rid of all that is best for them and then declare that they feel perfectly well! But they do not know how the laws operate.

They do not know that even if their affairs seem to be going very well for quite a long time, the slightest deviation on the philosophical level inevitably leads to a hopeless tangle of difficulties in the long run.

What you have to understand is that one cannot detach oneself or cut oneself off from anything or anyone — in the broad sense of the term — without, by that very fact, attaching oneself to something or someone else. One is always subject to an influence: the influence of the weather, the temperature, the times in which one lives — or the influence of the stars! One is obliged to eat and drink, to breathe and sleep, to wear clothes, to meet other people and to listen and talk to them, and in all these activities one is influenced by certain forces. A woman may want to leave her husband in order to be free, but shortly afterwards she finds herself involved with someone else, and her situation may well be worse. When ignorant, unsuspecting human beings start out in search of what they take to be freedom, there are always other forces waiting to catch them and drag them into their zone of influence.

Everything that exists both in us and around us has its own particular properties which we must learn to recognize. If you want to put out a fire — that is, a burning desire, a passion that is

consuming you — and you do not know any better, you might put coal or oil on it — symbolically
speaking — and then your fire will burn all the
more fiercely. That is the kind of thing most people do. If you want to get rid of something that is
troubling you, you have to find the element,
region, entity or virtue which has the qualities
needed to be helpful and effective, and if you
want to be free then you must be sure to find out
which element possesses that quality. Personally,
in my endeavour to find freedom, I have found
that nothing is more effective than to attach
myself to the Supreme Being.

Let me give you an example : suppose you are
working in a government office, and you have to
obey the slightest whim of those over you. If you
want to escape from that situation you know that
you will have to win promotion and rise to a
higher position than theirs. So you study as hard
as you can and pass all kinds of exams and you
end up as the head of the department, even above
your boss ! And, from then on, he cannot perse-
cute you any more. Of course, you will still have to
put up with others, in higher echelons, so perhaps
you will set out to climb even higher, above them
too. And, as there will always be someone above
you, you will keep climbing until you reach the
Lord Himself !

I have known a number of people who, on the pretext of seeking freedom, have abandoned their families, their work and their friends. Selling all their belongings, they left everything behind them and went to seek happiness in some other country. They did not know that one cannot find freedom that way. They freed themselves from external ties, perhaps, but they forgot to work on their inner reality, they forgot to free themselves from certain thoughts and desires, with the result that wherever they go they will always find themselves faced with the same difficulties. I have seen so many people in my life who have tried to free themselves, but they all go about it so clumsily, in ways that are dangerous for themselves and for others! I have always told them, 'Now look, suppose your house is old and tumbling down; it is very uncomfortable and you don't want to live in it any more. I quite understand; that's normal. But don't pull it down until you have built another one in its place, otherwise you'll be out on the street, at the mercy of the wind and rain — symbolically speaking? This is exactly what I mean when I tell you that before you can free yourselves from your present attachments, you have to attach yourselves to something new. This new attachment is the new, better house you have to build and, once you have built it, you will be free to pull down the old one. But you must not do it the other way round and detach yourself before you are safely attached to something else, otherwise your detachment will be useless; you will simply find yourself attached to all kinds of erratic elements and your situation will be even more painful than before. So remember: do not detach yourselves before attaching yourselves; do not destroy before you have built anew.

Now, one more example, just to show you that when I tell you something you can always find confirmation of the truth of it in all the manifestations of nature. Suppose you have cut yourself and, under the scab which has formed over the wound, a new skin is beginning to grow. If you scratch at the scab and pull it off before the new skin is fully formed, you will simply reopen the wound and then you will have to wait for the whole process to take place all over again. Before you pull off the scab you must 'build your new house', that is you must allow the new skin to form over the wound. If you were really observant you would see that the human organism, nature, trees, in fact everything in the universe except man, respects this order of things.

Human beings want to be free, but as they do not realize the danger of breaking away from old attachments before they have created new ones, they are always getting caught out by unexpected

difficulties. The thing is that if you do not take
care to ensconce higher realities in the places you
have cleared out in your heart and mind, all kinds
of other entities will slip in, and you will be in a
terrible fix. Your hearts and minds must be fully
occupied by a very lofty ideal, by all that is best,
most noble and most luminous. That is why Initiates teach their disciples always to give first place
to the Lord. Even if this seems utterly ridiculous
and in complete contradiction to all the modern
ideas, do it ; put the Lord firmly in first place.

Most educators do not know this law which
says that one should create new bonds before
detaching oneself from the old ones. Suppose, for
instance, that the parents of a young girl want to
detach her from a boy who has seduced her. If
they do not know how to go about it they will
criticize him and point out all his faults and fail-
ings, with the result that they will simply
strengthen their daughter's attachment to him.
They should say nothing, but make sure that the
girl meets other young men who are better-
looking, more intelligent and more honest and
altogether more suitable. The girl will realize for
herself that she has been blind and stupid and will
detach herself from her seducer. You have to show
people alternatives, lct them taste other realities,
and that is what I do.

I know very well that I could never detach you from certain habits or mental attitudes if I did not begin by attaching you to something else. That is why I put before you all the glories of Heaven and the beauty of the soul, the spirit and the sun; I want you to see for yourselves how beautiful it is and feel the need to attach yourselves to all that beauty. Later, when you look back at all the rest and realize where you have come from, you will see the horror of it and want to flee! One must always let people find out for themselves what is best.

I expect you remember the example which I have often given you. Suppose I go to see a friend who lives on a farm: it is winter and all the doors and windows are tightly shut and the stench is overpowering, because the cat and the dog and even the horses and pigs are all there too! It is more economical, you understand, everybody mucks in together and it's lovely and warm! Yes, but they have all become completely groggy from the fumes; they are incapable of thinking clearly about anything. So what do I do? If I tried to explain to them how unhealthy, offensive and unsightly their living habits were it would only trigger interminable discussions. They would have all kinds of arguments to prove that they

were in the right and I was in the wrong and I
would simply be wasting my time! So I use guile!
I invite them to go out for a walk with me, or to go
with me to pick up a parcel I had left somewhere,
and we all go out together into the fresh air for a
few minutes and when we go back into the house
it is they who exclaim in horror at the filth, and
wonder how they ever managed to live in such a
vile atmosphere, that is to say in such a vile
philosophy, with such inadequate understanding.
Ah, now they are beginning to understand me!

You see, it was they who understood for
themselves, they made the comparison instinc-
tively. It is quite possible that, as they left the
house, they did not realize at once how marvellous it was to breathe the pure fresh air, but when
we got back and they were suffocated by the
stench in the house, then they understood! Then I
could talk to them to some purpose and get
results, but not before. Before detaching them
from that poisonous atmosphere they had to be
attached to the pure air out of doors.

Anyone who does not understand this law
and who attempts to improve human beings
without first giving them a taste of something
better, something that makes them expand with
delight and wonder, something that makes them
feel the irresistible attraction of good, will fail in
his undertaking. It does absolutely no good to

rant and rave against evil if one does nothing to help people to see the beauty of good and be drawn to bind themselves to it so as to advance, for that is where freedom lies, in that attachment to good.

6

TRUE FREEDOM :
A CONSECRATION OF SELF

One of the rarest qualities to be found in human beings is tenacity: the capacity to maintain one's first enthusiasm for a magnificent, divine undertaking without ever giving way to discouragement. Unfortunately, many people, even amongst those who have embraced a lofty spiritual ideal, become discouraged. They start by making a few little efforts, by trying out some exercises, and then, when they fail to get the results they had hoped for, they give up. This only shows that they have not understood the true nature of spiritual work. In the spiritual life, whatever happens, you have to keep at it and one day, at long last, you will see the fruits of your work and reap an abundant harvest.

If a collectivity, a brotherhood, is useful and even indispensable for the progress of humanity it is because it gives people the ideal conditions in which to learn perseverance. When you are at

home, alone, you may be inspired by a book you
have been reading, and decide to change your way
of life, to practise certain exercises and so on, but
you will not keep it up for very long because there
is nothing to stimulate you to do so. Whereas in a
community like the Universal White Brotherhood, even if you are tired and discouraged and
ready to give it all up, when you see others per-
severing it helps you to regain courage and to keep
trying.

Except for a few, very exceptional cases,
human beings all need support and stimulation,
for there are always moments when one's ardour
flags. Of course, I know that some people will say
that they have no wish to be influenced, that they
want to do as they please when they please, and
that that is why they do not join a community:
they would find themselves too restricted. Well,
all I can say is that these people are not very intelligent. Someone who was intelligent would be
eager to put themselves in a position where they
would be prevented from doing something
stupid, and free, on the contrary, to launch into
all kinds of beneficial, luminous undertakings.

When you feel the urge to do something
foolish, instead of looking for conditions that
will make it easier for you, you should run for
shelter, run to somewhere where you will not be
able to commit your act of folly, or ask someone

to stop you. Suppose you feel the urge to murder someone: Quick! Run to a friend and ask him to tie you up! Of course, this is a rather extreme example, but there are a great many circumstances in which you can apply various forms of this method. You could go and talk to someone, or read a book which would influence you favourably and counteract the evil tendencies at work in you. But human beings have no idea when or how they should tie themselves up, nor when or how they should free themselves. In fact, you can only find true freedom when you know how, to what extent and when to limit yourself. This is why the only ones who are really free are Initiates: for years and years they limited themselves, learning renunciation and self-sacrifice, and now they are free.

Those who think that freedom consists in being totally independent of everything and everyone, do not realize how dangerous that attitude is: if they have nothing to fill their minds, their souls and their spirits it means that they are full of gaps, and all the spirits of darkness, all the negative, demonic entities roaming in search of shelter find those gaps and slip into them. These people seek freedom but in conditions that will inevitably lead to their being totally submerged by other forces of which they know nothing. I have so often seen this happening! I have seen women who were so hungry for money and the freedom to pursue pleasure and luxury, that they married rich men whom they did not love, without realizing that instead of finding freedom they would become the prisoners of others. Outwardly, perhaps, they found a certain freedom, but inwardly? Outward freedom is, more often than not, a false freedom.

The Devil soon finds work for anyone whose mind is not already occupied by a divine, sublime ideal: he encourages them to give a free rein to their passions and pushes them into all kinds of follies and wild adventures. And all this because they were free, unoccupied! The only way to be free and safe at the same time, is to be fully occupied, engaged, by Heaven. There is no such thing as a vacuum, and that is why you have to hurry to be free no longer by making yourself available to heavenly forces; otherwise you will be snapped up by the forces of Hell.

Human beings are halfway between a sublime world of harmony and light and another, dark, chaotic world. These two worlds, which we call Heaven and Hell are at war with each other in and through us and, in our ignorance, we allow the world of darkness to infiltrate our defences and set up camp within us. That is why we are constantly miserable, torn this way and that. The solution to the problem of freedom lies in a proper understanding of two processes: approach and withdrawal. We can find freedom only in a commitment, a total submission to Heaven, because the powers of Heaven never use coercion or constraint, on the contrary, they dispose and order everything in harmony and beauty.

Human beings value freedom so highly that they are ready to give their lives for it, but unfortunately they have not yet properly understood the nature of that freedom they cherish and pursue so ardently. No one wants to be subjugated by a foreign country, that is natural enough, but suppose that that country is Heaven — would it not be better to be invaded, dominated and ruled by such an intelligent country? You only have to look at what happens so often: a country struggles to free itself from the domination of a foreign power and as soon as it succeeds, its own supposedly free citizens start to dominate and subjugate each other and massacre their rivals! It is perfectly legitimate for a country to win and defend its independence, but it is not enough to envisage the question of freedom or liberty only on that level.

Freedom is something which concerns the inner life. A great many people are free outwardly but not inwardly, because they are besieged by thoughts and feelings which rob them of their freedom. Freedom should be thought of as an inner state of mind produced by certain thoughts and feelings. Certainly, it is very desirable to be physically free, but physical freedom should never go before inner freedom because it is often precisely when one is physically free that one gets caught in a snare. I have seen this so often!

You think you are free because you are not in prison and you are not a slave. Yes, but inwardly, are you not constantly forced to serve tyrants? If you would only analyse yourselves honestly you would be bound to admit that all the choices you have made, as you think, freely, were in fact dictated by certain desires or passions which dominate you and which you are unable to resist. So your freedom is all a fake! What tremendous struggles human beings have undertaken for the sake of social or political freedom! And what a pity that they have never spent so much energy or fought such valiant battles for spiritual freedom!

A great many people are like a horse tethered to a stake in the middle of a pasture: as long as it never tries to go beyond the limit imposed by the rope, it is free to move about, but if it wants to stray into greener pastures, the rope tightens round its neck and stops it. Similarly, when it comes to satisfying their physical appetites or their basest desires, these people do not feel tied, but if they wanted to reach higher, subtler, more spiritual regions, they would be obliged to recognize that they are limited, tied down and enslaved.

True freedom is not a question of not being bound by a rope. Every time you obey an inferior desire you demonstrate that you are a slave; and the world is full of slaves, poor, unhappy wretches, tossed to and fro, and who think that they can excuse all their faults and follies by saying, 'I couldn't help it!' When someone says that, it is obvious that he is already a slave; he is at the mercy of someone or something other than himself. A free man would never say 'I couldn't help it'. It is an admission of defeat; it is as though he showed you his visiting card with the description of his qualifications: 'Slave; weak; worthless'. 'Nonsense!' you will exclaim; 'My visiting card shows that I'm Chairman of this and Director of that..'. Yes? Well, that is perfectly possible, but what I read is something quite different. Is it my fault if I have been so conditioned by my work that I always read between — or behind — the lines?

The only kind of freedom which really exists is consecration. Before projecting forces onto an object which he intends to consecrate, an Initiate purifies and exorcizes it, freeing it from the influence of those who have already handled it, or of events which have taken place in its vicinity and left fluidic layers of impure, opaque matter on it. Otherwise these fluidic layers could form a barrier, an obstructive screen, which would bar his magic thought from impregnating the object. Only after the object has been exorcized by suitable formulae and the scent of incense, will the Initiate consecrate it to an Entity, a Principle or a Virtue so that it becomes reserved, set apart. It is as though it were protected by a sign: 'Private property. Keep out!' It is steeped in good influences, and evil spirits cannot get into it or use it for their own ends.

Nature has many laws and interdictions which even evil spirits recognize and respect because they know that if they disobey certain rules they will be punished. But, naturally, when the way is wide open to them, even God Himself cannot forbid them to go in to hunt for food and to ransack and foul everything. They are within their rights; the door was open. Some Christians wonder why God allows evil spirits to get in to them. What a stupid question! If they do nothing to defend themselves why should God defend them? There are laws and rules in this respect and you must know them. If there were no wall round your orchard to keep people out, would you be surprised to find that it had been ransacked? Of course not! In fact, if you appealed to a court of law you would certainly be told that you should have put up a fence to show that it was private property. If there was no fence, the law can do nothing about it.

Oh, yes. Everybody wants to be free, free — but free from what ? Free from whom ? Free from Instructors who would teach them wisdom and awaken their higher consciousness ? Free from the Lord ? Free from Heaven ? But if that is what they want, then they are already available to the powers of Hell who will waste no time in filling them with all kinds of insane, criminal ideas. They are surrounded by hostile forces just waiting to lead them astray and amuse themselves at their expense ; and in the end their reward is illness and suffering. All these so-called 'free' people have a great emptiness inside them and, of course, evil thoughts, feelings and entities roaming through the world, see this and go in to look for food. Like wild animals, they need to eat, and they fall upon the first victim that comes their way ; if he cannot defend himself he will be devoured. Every creature, everything in life needs to nourish itself, and evil creatures are ready to fall upon anything and anyone in order to eat. You only have to see how microbes, bacilli and viruses behave : the law is the same on every level.

If a man does not have the sense to defend himself, he will be invaded by negative forces and then he will lament and wail and wring his hands

in despair — and never understand what has happened to him or why! And yet, isn't it quite easy
to understand? He has been too credulous; he
did not realize that he should not leave himself
empty and exposed, his doors and windows wide
open to all the ne'er-do-wells of the invisible
world who feed on human beings.

You all know how hunters behave: they go
out with guns and dogs to shoot birds or animals
which they then eat or sell or use to show off in
front of others. Well, that is exactly what these
mischievous entities of the invisible world do:
they go hunting for some toothsome human
game and then they eat the ones they catch! So
you must be occupied, inhabited, committed, but
by Heaven and the Angels and Archangels. It is
this submission to the sublime powers above
which enables you to be absolutely free, because
they will never plunder you; on the contrary. As
they are rich, intelligent and full of beauty and
light, they bring all their treasures, all their splendour with them and share them with you. So it is
far better to be occupied, engaged and con-
secrated in this way than to be stupidly available,
'free'. True freedom consists in not being free!

How many boys and girls want to be free to
'live their own lives!' But what kind of lives can
they live if they have neither science, nor learning,

neither light nor willpower? They will live like animals: eating and quarrelling, laughing and crying, and then laughing again and crying again. That is how one 'lives one's own life'. You must not delude yourself that you are free just because you can do what you please and go wherever you like without a guide and without an ideal. If you do not consecrate your life to Heaven, freedom is simply a form of slavery.

What I have just explained to you about the exorcism which has to be done before a rite of consecration can take place, is of immeasurable importance in understanding this question of freedom. If you learn how to apply it to yourself, you can surround and protect yourself by magic circles of light; heavenly spirits will be attracted by your aura and will come and guard you and keep all unwelcome visitors away. But you must work and be constantly occupied, you must keep busy! Look at what happens to so many people when they retire: they suddenly start to get old much more quickly. I have nothing against retiring from work, but you have to use your retirement to do another kind of work, a gigantic spiritual work. Ah, if you do that, you will be sustained and revivified and find yourself getting younger again!

Every day you should repeat this prayer: 'Lord God, accept me as your servant, I am yours to do what you like with; guide me, work through me for the fulfilment of all your plans? Obviously, you will not notice any fantastic results in the first few days! But in the long run you will see: you will feel so powerfully guided, sustained and protected, so full of light and joy that words will be powerless to describe it! So, there you are: never be free! And don't delay: hurry to have done with your own little freedom, and implore Heaven to come and take possession of you today!

This is one of the greatest secrets of Initiation!

7

FREEDOM THROUGH SELF-LIMITATION

The goal of most oriental spiritual teachings is liberation. For thousands of years, the Initiates of India, Tibet and Japan have worked to find methods which would enable them to free themselves from the bonds holding them down to earth. This is why many of them retired into caves or deep into the forest in order to devote themselves wholly to this work of liberation. Personally, I do not like that attitude much; it still seems rather selfish to me. Why try to free oneself? I have no desire to be free, on the contrary, I want to limit myself and consciously commit myself. If you are so intent on freeing yourself then, of course, it only remains for you to walk out on everything and everyone: nothing else matters. It must be fine to be free and to float in light, bliss and ecstasy, to know the beatitude of Nirvana, but personally, I cannot see any advantage in being happy all alone; that is not what I want. And that is why I have limited myself and committed myself totally. I came down to earth because I thought it was selfish to stay up there, in such freedom and happiness. I understood that it would be better to come here and be knocked about and criticized and dirtied. But perhaps you will complain that you do not understand what I am talking about. Have a little patience and you will soon understand.

When a being has become totally free and paid all his debts, he no longer needs to reincarnate. He can stay up above in heavenly bliss and light, with no obligations to drag him back to earth. But every now and then, amongst all those who have already attained freedom, there is one who sees how much human beings are suffering and decides to help them. He requests an audience with the Twenty-four Elders and asks them for permission to return to earth, and the Twenty-four Elders examine the question. Naturally, they want to make the most of this extraordinary opportunity: someone who is ready to sacrifice himself! And as they are an expression of the unfathomable wisdom of Almighty God, they plan the most terrible and, at the same time, the most marvellous experiences for the life of that being on earth. Then, before he reincarnates, they show him all these events and experiences as in a film, and ask him if he is ready to accept all that. And, of course, he does accept.

It is almost as though many of those who have completed their evolution on this planet tired of all that joy and happiness, all that light. Even some of the very greatest Initiates who have lived on earth seem unable to wipe out the memory of that experience and sever their bonds with the earth. They are free, they have been victorious in all their battles, they are living in eternity and yet, from time to time, they feel the desire to gaze on those poor human beings amongst whom they lived and with whom, in spite of the great distance between them, they still feel a bond. Centuries, even millenaries after leaving the earth, they still remember, and in the greatness, the abundance and the tremendous love of their hearts, they decide to come down and help humanity. And that is what I did.

You have to free yourself, that is true, but in order to limit yourself. You have to free yourself inwardly from all your lower instincts and tendencies in order to bind yourself to something higher, to working for the collectivity. That, for me, is the true meaning of life and liberty. Happiness and joy consist in freeing oneself, not in shirking one's obligations, but in freeing oneself inwardly from all one's weaknesses in order to commit oneself even more wholeheartedly to helping others. Yes, if you want to be inwardly free, you have to begin by limiting yourself and sacrificing certain things in order to commit yourself more fully.

How can anyone who is not free commit himself to a divine task? This is quite obvious to me: those who are not free cannot be very useful because they are busy serving other gods — and believe me, there are quantities of other gods! They are not free because ever since they were young they have cherished all sorts of plans and personal goals, and their first priority has been to fulfil these ambitions. The result is that they are now so deeply involved elsewhere that they have no time to give to the collectivity. What can you do if you are not free? Even if you do come and listen to one of my lectures, you will not understand it if your mind is not free, if you are assailed by all kinds of bizarre thoughts and feelings and memories.

In fact if I were to ask you, 'What is the difference between a spiritual Master and a university professor of any discipline you like?' I am certain you would not know what to answer. Perhaps you would say, 'Well, it's the type of knowledge, the syllabus and the goal they pursue..' Yes, that is certainly true. But there is a much more important difference, and you have not mentioned it because you have never thought about it. I'll tell you: once a university professor has completed his course of lectures he can forget about his students. He has enough concerns of his own to occupy him: his personal problems, his private thoughts, feelings and suffering. Once he has given his course his job is finished. Whereas a Master's work is never finished; he never puts aside his concern for his disciples. Night and day, eating, working or sleeping, he never relaxes his care for the souls and spirits of his disciples; ceaselessly, every moment of every day he is at their side, helping them. Yes, a Master, an Initiate is free. And when someone is free and has solved all his own personal problems, he can help his friends, disciples and pupils. Whereas if one is forever embroiled in a tangle of personal problems, as most human beings are, what can one do for others? There, now you see the difference between an authentic spiritual Master and an ordinary instructor: a Master is free!

Everyone thinks that the spiritual Teachings of the East are marvellous — and you are no exception! But do you realize that if I followed them it would mean that I would abandon you and devote myself to my own spiritual work? And tell me: would you be pleased if I abandoned you? By committing myself more and more

deeply I am reaching greater and greater freedom. That is quite a new aspect of the question,
isn't it? Spiritual people who are only interested
in their own, personal liberation are all in error;
there is no love in that attitude. It is sheer selfish-
ness! The time has come, now, to put the empha-
sis on collective work, for it is through work that
one attains freedom. For my part, this is how I
have resolved the problem: I don't want to be free,
I want to do the work that needs to be done, and it
is in that work that I find all my delight.

If you want to be strong in life you have to
impose certain limitations on yourself. If you
scatter a handful of gunpowder on the ground
and throw a lighted match on it, it will just go
'pfft' and fizzle out because it had too much free
space. But if you pack it tightly into a shell case
and then touch off the detonator, it will explode
with a roar and demolish everything around it.
Human beings are like gunpowder: they have to
be compressed before they feel the urge to burst
out and conquer the world. If a man has too
much free space he will never do anything. Freedom often chloroforms people and puts them to
sleep and they never do anything useful any
more: they are too free! That is why Cosmic
Intelligence packs some people into terribly tight
situations, so as to get them to set the whole world
ablaze! These are things you have to think about.

I am not saying that one should always be hemmed in, exploited and ground underfoot, no! But I am saying that this question of freedom is not quite as simple as you might think. When one has never had any instruction in Initiatic Science one can have a very mistaken outlook; it is not easy to understand why one has to put up with certain circumstances and it is not easy to distinguish the good from the bad side of a given situation. Someone who is very well off on the material level, for instance, may think that he is in a privileged position: he does not realize the dangers of his situation. For him, what counts is the external aspect. The fact is that there is always a good and a bad side to everything: think about that. Even if you cannot immediately find the significance of a situation in which you are struggling, the simple fact that you use your mind to think about it is already something — in fact it is a great deal!

In my own life I have found that difficult conditions have been enormously helpful in stimulating reflection. If I had not encountered, very early on in life, conditions which seemed, on the surface, to be utterly deplorable and miserable, I would never have discovered or achieved anything. That is why I thank Heaven for all the privations, difficulties and misfortunes I have received. Yes, really! I thank Heaven for them!

Once one has understood one can see the good
side of these things. And I am saying this for you,
too, so that when you find yourself obliged to live
through something very difficult you may not be
discouraged but, on the contrary, that you may
recognize the good side and learn, as I have, to
thank Heaven every day for the trials and tribula-
tions you have had to live through. Before rebel-
ling against your lot, think, reflect and meditate
and you will certainly discover a great deal about
the usefulness of these trials. For my part I am
continually making new discoveries in this
respect!

There are a great many qualities that one
would never develop if one did not have to
experience certain trials. And, in fact, I would go
so far as to say that our enemies are often friends
in disguise, because they oblige us to exert ourselves and it is the efforts we make which liberate
us. That is why we must love our enemies. Jesus
said, 'Love your enemies.' Yes, that is really
meritorious. It is too easy to love your friends;
anyone can do that. But it is very difficult to love
one's enemies. In fact one can only love them if
one realizes that they are friends in disguise,
thanks to whom we are making great strides on
the path towards self-mastery and liberation.

Isn't life beautiful? When you know that
you can love even your enemies and that hidden

behind all the most unfortunate circumstances are the greatest possible blessings, how can you avoid rejoicing? Once one has understood that, one is free. Yes, free! But free to chain oneself all the more securely to the divine work.

8

ANARCHY AND FREEDOM

In their eagerness to be free, people move farther and farther away from the Source without realizing that in so doing they are accepting slavery and lies. They justify all their aberrations by declaring with pride: 'To each his own truth' or 'There's no accounting for taste!' In fact, they even say this in Latin, just to make it sound wiser and more philosophical: *'De gustibus et coloribus non disputandum.'* And all it means is that there is no universal norm, that each person must be allowed to have his favourite folly and the right to abandon himself to whatever depravity his folly may lead to.

But I say, 'No! There are universal norms which should govern our tastes; good and beauty should be good and beautiful to everyone.' Man's freedom in this area extends only to the question of quantity, not to quality. Anything else is no longer freedom but anarchy.

A great many people nowadays have embarked on this philosophical path of anarchy without realizing the dangers that lie along the way. Sooner or later they are bound to be destroyed. If they had studied the laws of Nature and the pattern on which the universe is built, all the regions of which it is composed and the multitudes of creatures who people these regions, they would have understood that they, too, are an integral part of the living body of Nature and must behave in such a way as to be in harmony with the whole. If their anarchical attitude becomes too troublesome to Nature, she has a simple and radical solution to hand: she takes a purge and flushes them out of her system. Anarchists are never tolerated for very long. If they are not exterminated by their fellow human beings, Nature takes care of them herself, for she cannot bear disharmony, it is like a tumour, a cancerous growth in her system and she does whatever she has to to eliminate it.

You will find all this written in the great Book of Living Nature. Once an Initiate has understood this truth, the thing he fears most is to become a tumour in the Cosmic Body because he failed to vibrate in unison. An Initiate fears nothing and nobody except this: to find himself psychically out of tune with the laws of the universe, because he knows what to expect if this were to happen. So he endeavours to conform and be always in unison with the great Cosmic Body.

If a singer in a choir or a player in an orchestra refuses to sing or play what is in the score, he is dismissed because he is destroying the harmony of the whole. That is exactly what happens to anarchists, and if they do not know it, it is because they are the blindest and most ignorant of men. If they had any intelligence at all they would realize that they could not have the upper hand for long, for they are always in danger of coming up against others, even more anarchical than themselves, and then it is they who will be the underdog! But, as I say, if they are not destroyed by other human beings they will be destroyed by Nature, for her laws are terrible and inexorable.

Now, let me make quite clear what I mean by 'anarchy'. What some people would call anarchy need not necessarily be considered bad. In theory, it is the state of mind of someone who intends to live his own life in his own way, even if his way runs counter to the established order. Whether that order be good or bad is all the same to him: he is going to live according to his own conceptions. Now, suppose that the person in question is an exceptionally exalted being: it could be that his conception of things is far more perfect than that of the establishment. Society may call him an anarchist, but in the eyes of Heaven he is no anarchist because his one desire is for greater love, brotherhood and justice. In the judgment of the Initiates, an anarchist is one who refuses to acknowledge the existence of a divine order, of a Supreme Lord of the Universe, of entities and forces superior to himself and of rules which command his obedience. Someone who lives in perfect conformity and harmony with a society of several millions of people who have absolutely no notion of spiritual life, may yet be considered an anarchist by Cosmic Intelligence because he transgresses the laws of God.

Just as long as your final goal is not Heaven itself, you are living in anarchy, even if you declare yourself to be completely opposed to it. It may be true that you are opposed to it on the intellectual level, but you are still living in anarchy, for what is your goal in life? And even if your ultimate goal is Heaven, have you mobilized all your energies to attain your goal? No! A great many of you roam in other pastures and dine at many other tables. To an Initiate, therefore, the situation looks quite different, because he can see all those elements within you which have still not been coordinated and brought into line.

In point of fact, although they do not know it, the majority of human beings are anarchists.

Outwardly they live decent, respectable lives, so decent and respectable, in fact, that some of them get decorated for it! They never break any man-made laws but inwardly they flout all the laws. They abide by society's laws because they are afraid of being criticized or arrested and condemned, but they have no such respect for the divine laws: if only they could understand that, in fact, the divine laws they flout so lightheartedly are far more to be feared than the laws of man! Anyone who is clever enough, or simply lucky enough, can always avoid being caught out by human laws, whereas no one has ever been intelligent or sly enough to escape the laws of God. The reason is that there is a higher Intelligence, far higher and greater than our own little human intelligence, which watches and records everything that happens. This is why evil-doers are always caught and punished. Without realizing it they always leave clues to their identity on the scene of the crime. Even thoughts or passing feelings leave a trace on the invisible level. If you go somewhere one day and, without actually committing a crime, you indulge in evil, poisonous thoughts, those thoughts leave their imprint on you and all round you. And that is why the law has to prosecute you: the divine law, I mean. Before too long, in one way or another, you will begin to feel the consequences of those thoughts.

According to Initiatic Science, an anarchist is someone who refuses to submit to the divine order, and that being so, one could say that nine tenths of humanity can be classed as anarchists! Usually, anarchy is defined according to social or political criteria, but that is totally inadequate: the only anarchy which really deserves the name is anarchy in the face of Heaven. Of course, many people are doubly anarchical: with regard to Heaven and with regard to earth!

You remember the parable of the Prodigal Son in the Gospel: he left his father's house and went to look for adventure in the world because he was bored at home and wanted to be free. To begin with, the novelty of his situation enchanted him but, gradually, things began to be more and more difficult. He was a foreigner in a strange land; people distrusted him; he was refused work. The wretched young man began to suffer real privations: he was hungry, thirsty and cold, for he had nowhere to live, and he began to long to be back home in his father's house where he could have everything he needed, where his father and mother and the whole family loved him, and all the neighbours knew him; so he decided to return home. And that is how, one day, wiser and humbler, ill, sorrowful and dressed in filthy rags, having learned to his cost that the world is ruled by neither love nor pity, he arrived on his father's doorstep, where his father greeted him with open arms. The story of this prodigal son is the story of every being who, instead of living in harmony with the divine laws, is bent on doing exactly as he pleases and lives in anarchy.

But, as I have said, the worst form of anarchy is that which is inside us. This is why the goal of Initiatic schools is to help people to turn round and start going back to their Father's house, to the safety of that 'Secret Place of the Most High' mentioned in Psalm 91, where the forces of evil cannot reach them. It always seems as though people were happy to leave that Secret Place where they are under God's protection; they want to get away from Him to live their own lives and break His laws. Well, all I can say is that there is still a great deal of suffering in store for people like that. That is why they have this perpetual tendency to step out of line, to refuse to obey: because it is written in their destiny that they have to suffer. Whereas those who have already suffered greatly and have understood, want nothing more than to return to the Father, to dwell in His peace and light.

Christ said, 'I am the vine, you are the branches. He who abides in me, and I in him, bears much fruit; for without me you can do nothing. If anyone does not abide in me, he is cast out as a branch and is withered; and they gather

them and throw them into the fire, and they
are burned? This is exactly the same idea, and
most human beings are branches which have been
cut off from the trunk; they wanted to cut
themselves off from the Lord in the hope
of getting some advantage, something that, in
fact they will never get. Before running off
like that, blindly, wouldn't it be far better to
study the laws and see in advance how events
are liable to turn out. Look at the prodigal son:
he should have examined the kind of life he
was living at home and compared it with that
which was waiting for him in the world, where
men survive only by using brute force against
each other. But the poor fellow did not take
the trouble to study the matter; he simply built
up a fantasy in his own imagination. Yes, well,
all anarchists do that! That is why I advise all
those who have embarked on the path of
anarchy to take a long hard look at what is in
store for them if they continue.

So many people imagine that by cultivat-
ing this attitude of anarchy and rebellion they
are showing their strength of character. On
the contrary, they are simply showing how
ignorant they are, for they are treading the road
that leads straight to dislocation and impo-
tence. Man's true strength and true liberation
lie in harnessing all his instinctive energies

and tendencies in one irresistible thrust towards Heaven, towards spiritual perfection.

This question of law is really not difficult to understand! Take any example from everyday life. Let's say, for instance, that you have over-eaten: there is no man-made law that forbids you to do so; there is no danger that a policeman will come and arrest you for gluttony! True, but you will be ill! So what is this system of justice which intervenes and sends you to bed with a bilious attack? The laws of Nature are not those of men. Your friends will come and sympathize with you: 'Poor old man! It's too bad that you're in such a state!' But they will not be able to do anything to help; only Nature can help you, and she will do so only if you obey her laws once again: then you will be cured. You must learn the laws of Nature, the divine laws that govern our minds and hearts and physical bodies. You must realize that whenever you say or do something, you are put-ting out energy and you must be careful to see where those energies are going and make sure that they are not doing any damage anywhere.

In the Tales from the Thousand and One Nights, there is the story of a traveller who sat down to rest under a tree. While he was sitting in the shade he ate some dates and carelessly threw the seeds on the ground around him. He had barely finished eating when a terrifying genie

appeared to him, announcing that he was going
to kill him. 'But, why?' said the man, 'What have
I done?' "You have been eating dates and throw-
ing away the seeds, and you wounded my son in
the eye as he was passing by, and he died. So now
it's your turn to die."' Of course, this is only a
fairy tale, but there is a lot of sense in it. Man is
never sufficiently aware of how much damage he
can do in both the visible and the invisible worlds.

Do as you please; put all the distance you
want between yourself and the Lord; be independent, and you will see how things turn out for
you. I already know what will happen. How?
Because it is very easy to understand what makes
someone adopt that attitude. Do you think that
someone who separates himself from God and
refuses to live in the light is motivated by any very
noble intentions? Not a bit of it! His goal is as
ordinary as can be: he wants to be rich, famous
and influential, and be able to eat, drink and for-
nicate to his heart's content! That is not a very
lofty ideal, is it? He is down there, rooting about
in the lower regions, and all he will ever dig up will
be suffering and unhappiness. I can tell exactly
what a man's future will be simply by knowing
what his ideal in life is: he will end up on the same
level as his ideal. When one possesses the Initiatic
Science it is easy to prophesy. When you know

what rails a train is running on, you can tell exactly what route it will follow and where it will end up. So you see : stationmasters are prophets ! And astronomers, too, because they can foretell the position of a planet years in advance ! In fact, anyone who has any sound scientific knowledge is a prophet : foreknowledge of the future is based on knowledge of the laws.

You must understand, henceforth, that a philosophy which estranges you from God will end by shackling and enslaving you completely, for there is no freedom to be found far from God. What would you expect to find if you moved farther from the sun ? Darkness, bitter cold and death ! But human beings never seem to understand this ; they are like children. When a child wants to be free it is because he wants to do all kinds of foolish or dangerous things, without realizing that those things will impose other limitations on him. The young — and adults, too, for that matter — have no more understanding of freedom than babies. Only a Sage knows that if you want to be free, you have to impose limits on yourself. Others, arguing that they are acting in the name of freedom, simply let loose ravening beasts — the destructive entities of the astral dimension — which end by demolishing and devouring them completely.

Yesterday I happened to switch on the television, just to see what was going on, and what did I see! Four hairy ruffians with faces like animals, screaming and gesticulating. It was a concert, apparently! Never have I heard such jarring, unbearable cacophony! But the young people in the audience were wildly enthusiastic: jumping up and down, twisting and contorting themselves and screaming their applause. And I was there, feeling such sadness as I watched, and I thought to myself, 'Dear Lord, how can anyone understand human nature? What can have happened in man's soul to have cut him off so completely from true beauty?' Four wild barbarians! And they are enormously popular! And it is not that I am so terribly severe or narrow-minded; I do not condemn young people because they need to let off steam to express their vitality and joy. But there was not even any joy there! And as for vitality, it was expressing itself in the most repulsive, dislocated, ungainly movements. Wild beasts! Yes, I saw them, there, on the stage: the cages were wide open and the wild beasts were everywhere, devouring every last scrap of good in those young men. And the audience was applauding the spectacle!

When I witnessed that I must say I almost despaired of guiding human beings to a goal of beauty and reason. They will have to go to the bitter end of the path they are on until they touch bottom. How can you expect people like that to understand the grandeur of the laws of creation and of Nature? They have never done any work on themselves; they don't even know that there is any work to do. The only thing they know is how to let the wild beasts out of their cages; that is all. And they call that freedom! Oh, yes; they are free and independent all right: unleashed!

9

THE NOTION OF HIERARCHY

The Book of Genesis tells the story of Jacob, who went to sleep one night with his head on a stone, and while he slept he had a vision of a ladder reaching from earth to Heaven, and on the ladder were angels, ascending and descending. This was how Jacob received the revelation of that great heavenly hierarchy which links earth to Heaven.

Jacob's ladder is the symbol of the angelic order of beings which is the link between man and God and which is represented in cabbalistic tradition by the Tree of Life or Sephirotic Tree. Anyone who imagines that man can converse directly with God, as many Protestants believe, only shows how ignorant he is. Here, on earth, there is no way of getting an audience with an important person without the assistance of all kinds of intermediaries, so how can anyone possibly imagine that he can have direct access to Almighty God and not

be struck down as though by lightning? Many
people seem to picture the Lord as a kind old gen-
tleman who is always ready to chat with them or
to have his beard pulled! In reality, the Lord is a
'power station' of such 'high voltage' that if
there were no 'transformers', that is no hierarchy
between man and God, anyone who got anywhere
near Him would disappear without a trace.

   If human beings possess this notion of hierarchy in their ordinary way of life, it is because it
has been communicated to them by Cosmic Intelligence who designed and implanted the hierarchical structure not only in the vast universe but
also within man's physical body. Man's body is
composed of a skeletal structure which corresponds to the mineral realm and which, like the
minerals of the earth, provides a material foundation. The muscles of the body are attached to
the skeleton, just as vegetation is attached to the
ground. The blood vessels of the circulatory system correspond to the rivers and oceans on earth,
for water is the blood of the planet which conveys
food to the vegetation. Man's respiratory system
corresponds to the air we breathe and, finally, the
nervous system corresponds to the sun which has
priority over all the other components. It is not a
man's bones, therefore, which are in command,
but the subtlest and most highly developed component in his makeup, his nervous system. Why

has nobody ever drawn the obvious philosophical conclusion from this and understood that we must give priority to the spirit?

A hierarchy is an ascending scale on which those in the lower positions are subject to those above them. This notion of hierarchy is so deeply ingrained in nature that even animals respect it: they always choose the strongest, most intelligent or most handsome amongst them as their leader. In the forest, the wild stag lords it over a few does: he is the leader and all the others obey him. When another stag comes along, the old stag fights to keep control of his females and his territory, but if the young intruder defeats him then it is he who becomes the new leader. Even wild animals know that worth must be recognized and respected, but human beings have lost their sense of worth because of their pride. You see, there is another definition of humility for you: to acknowledge the existence of a hierarchy. If you are capable of recognizing superiority where it really is, then you are humble.

Wherever you go throughout the world or beyond it, in the farthest reaches of outer space, however many celestial schools you attend, you will find this notion of hierarchy established everywhere: at the summit is God, the Lord and Ruler of all, and below Him are His servants whose mission is to carry out His orders, each in his own place. And when you succeed in establishing this hierarchy within yourself, then everything functions smoothly and in perfect harmony.

So you have to understand that when I insist so strongly on this notion of hierarchy, it is, above all, that inner hierarchy that I have in mind, that organization in which God presides over the whole. A man may be outwardly at the head of his company or his country, and yet be a complete nonentity inwardly. In society it is possible for a man to reach the top simply because he is rich or learned, but in the eyes of the divine world, the first place is for those who have far more important qualities than wealth or learning. As a matter of fact, it is quite easy to see this: you will never get your inner forces and entities to obey you if you are not above them. They know, they can feel immediately and infallibly who you are and what you are worth, and if you are not their superior they will refuse to obey you! Even if you try to order them to do things in the name of Jesus, they will reply, 'Right, we know who Jesus is, but who are you?' Not only will they refuse to obey you but they will knock you down and trample on you!

Why do all human beings, all over the world, do all they can to move up in rank or social standing? Because they know that if they had a higher position they would also earn more money and people would tip their hats to them — and instead of riding a bicycle they would drive a car! Ah, yes, it is all a question of position! Everyone knows that, and everyone tries to apply it in his own case, but only a tiny minority has understood that if we want to command the respect and obedience of our unruly population of cells, we have to make the effort to move up to a higher position inwardly also.

Look at the policeman directing the traffic: all he has is his uniform and a pair of white gloves, but he only has to wave his hand and everyone obeys him. He only has to say, 'Move along!' and everyone moves, even ministers and university professors! He may be almost illiterate but he has his uniform, his badge and his white gloves, and that is all he needs to keep order. And isn't it the same within yourself? If you wear a special 'uniform' or 'badge' your 'citizens' will be duly impressed and hasten to obey you. One word from you and they all murmur 'Amen'. Every time you move one step upwards in purity, self-mastery or discernment, therefore, new and marvellous horizons open up before you.

But, as I have just said, you must understand that when I speak of the hierarchy, I mean our inner hierarchy. Once that hierarchy is firmly established within you, you are free. You are king of your own kingdom, you can reclaim your throne and command obedience from all your subjects : feelings, thoughts, instincts and desires. For some people, freedom means opening the prison door and running out, crying 'Freedom at last !' without realizing that there are many different kinds of prison and they are all within them, not on the outside. No, he who gives first place to his impulses and passions is a slave and his desire for freedom is focussing on the wrong target. In fact, only the spirit is free, so only he in whom the spirit rules — that is, he who gives priority to the light and to all that is highest and most noble and just — has the right to be free. When someone like this appears, those around him sense that they can trust him and they begin to follow him, and he wins both freedom and authority amongst men, but not before he has won them within himself first.

Start concentrating on this notion of a hierarchy which extends all the way to the Throne of God, and ask yourself how you can establish it within yourself. You must pray and implore and struggle until the Spirit of God, the sublime Head of this hierarchy, comes to dwell in you and transforms everything. When He comes, in a flash, everything within you starts vibrating in harmony and joy. But without the head there is nothing you

can do; if there is no head there is no hierarchy!
The head is all-important. You do have the power
to transform everything within you, movements,
currents and forces, yes: but only by changing the
head, by establishing the Lord at the head of your
hierarchy.

So a hierarchy is an ascending scale in which
those who are on the lower rungs are subject to
those above them and in which the activities of
each one converge at the summit. This notion of
convergence is of prime importance. Take the
example of a tree: where is the head of a tree? You
will probably tell me that it is at the top, but no, it
is not! The head of a tree is its roots. In relation to
man a tree is upside down, its head is below, hidden under the earth. If the branches, leaves,
flowers and fruit of a tree are not connected to the
roots, the tree withers and dies. This is the very
same image that Jesus gave when he spoke of the
vine and its branches. The vine is the part that is
permanently in the soil, whereas the leaves and
flowers appear only periodically.

In man, too, there is a hierarchy which starts
at his feet and reaches up to his brain. If the whole
is to be harmoniously balanced and coordinated,
pulling all together towards a single goal, all the
different organs must be united in their submission to something which represents the summit
(or, if you prefer: the centre; the idea is the same).

Unity depends on this and unity is the primary condition for life. If the planets did not rotate round the sun, if they spun out of orbit into space and severed their links with the sun, it would mean their death because they would no longer be able to receive its light and warmth. Similarly, as everything in the universe is constructed on the same pattern, if the organs and cells of a man's body are not linked to his spirit, to his divine Self, as the planets are linked to the sun, they too will know weakness and disease and, eventually, dislocation and death. This is a truth which Initiates see reflected in every area of nature.

If you keep this picture constantly before you of a hierarchy which reaches from the rocks of the earth all the way up to God Himself, you will begin to feel that every part of you is becoming more coordinated and organized. For a hierarchy is a state of perfect harmony in which everything fits into its own place. Yes, everyone and everything in its proper place: that is the hierarchy, and it applies in every domain. Unfortunately this is not what we see in present-day society, in which the best and most intelligent people are often unknown or despised and the first places are filled by the violent, the avaricious and the cunning. But, as I have said, it is not so much the outward, social hierarchy which interests me as the inner hierarchy. It may well be that the first places in society can be had by trampling on, or even liquidating others: there have been enough instances of this in the records of wars and revolutions. But in the spiritual world these methods are worse than useless: the only way to succeed is by constant, tenacious work. That is the only way to move up the hierarchical ladder and gain authority not only over one's own, inner forces, but over the forces of nature: with this method, one day, one can become a divinity.

This is the law: human beings may only receive as much as they deserve but they will receive all they deserve. This law, which was promulgated by the Twenty-four Elders, applies universally. The heavenly entities know exactly what you are worth, what you are capable of achieving, and they arrange things in such a way that, eventually, you receive exactly what you deserve. But as most human beings do not know these laws, and do not believe that there are highly intelligent beings over us who are just, clairvoyant and faithful to the law, they use violence, cruelty and deceit to get what they want and then, of course, the forces of nature have to administer the lessons they deserve.

No one can take the place of another. Every single person in the universe has his own place, designated by God, with its own particular vibrations. On the physical plane, to be sure, people who are dishonest and unjust can evict others and supplant them, but on the spiritual level no one can ever take another's place from him. The place given to us by God is absolutely the place he deserves on the hierarchical ladder. In this area, absolute justice reigns; injustice cannot exist. No, no one can substitute for another, but each individual has to grow and develop until he reaches the place that God has designed for him. And once he has developed fully in accordance with God's design, then he will be unique and irreplaceable for eternity. No one else in the whole universe will be exactly like him. Even though others may be more important in the over-all scheme of things, in his own sphere it is he who will reign, for God has given him that sphere as his own. Every creature, by the life it lives, secretes a specific quintessence, and even if another rises to a higher level, each retains its own quintessence for they are of a different nature. No one creature, therefore, can supplant or substitute itself for another.

It is often the best people who appear to be victims of injustice, but if they are truly the best and do not give way to discouragement in the face of all the difficulties they encounter, heaven and earth have sworn to reward them as they deserve. This has always been so for every human being, and it will continue to be so for all eternity. And of course this means that we need not worry our heads about whether the entities of the invisible world are intelligent or if they have gone to sleep and forgotten us! The only thing we need to worry about is to do our own work properly; those entities are well aware how to do theirs, and when the time comes they will give us the royal reward we have merited.

Imagine the case of the young prince who, while still a child, had been put in the care of a peasant family to be brought up in a simple, even harsh, way of life. He has no idea that he is heir to the throne and he goes to work every day, clad in rags and with only just enough to eat. Then, one day, when he has completed several years of hard apprenticeship, a sumptuous procession of courtiers arrives to fetch him and take him away with them in a splendid coach. He does not understand what is happening; he is sure it is all a mistake. But no! he had been sent away from court to learn to work hard, get up early and live soberly. Because, as you all know, when a royal child is brought up in luxury, he often grows up to be capricious, lazy and cruel. So, our young prince arrives at the royal palace and when his courtiers ask him what he would like for lunch he asks for bread, an onion, some cheese and a glass of water! Well, you can imagine the despair of his

courtiers: what are they going to say to the royal
chef who has prepared a magnificent feast with
turkeys and lobsters and the very best wines! And
now, suppose I tell you that you are all, every one
of you, royal princes and princesses, sons and
daughters of God who has put you in the care of
peasants — symbolically speaking — to be
brought up by them, and that one day God will
send a solemn delegation to take you home. Yes,
but only on condition that you have worked well,
otherwise you may well have to go on with your
apprenticeship for centuries!

The thing that is essential, therefore, is to
install a new head inside oneself, because then
everything will be changed. But human beings
have still not understood how important the head
is. And yet, every one knows that when a new
President is elected, the whole government
changes and new ministers and a whole new
organization are put in place. Why is this? Why
don't they keep the same people in power?
Because it would be utterly impossible: the law of
affinity and magnetic attraction demands that
there be a new hierarchy, a new order. If a gangster gets elected he gives all the key posts to his
thugs, and disorder and injustice become the rule.
You have all noticed how these things change,
haven't you? As soon as a new man is in place, the
old staff is fired and new people who have an

affinity with the new leader, his supporters, friends and family, are given the best jobs.

So why try to make out that a new head will not make any difference, that things will always be the same? No, no! Everything will be changed, because the key posts will be given to people who agree with the head. So, if the head is a gangster, all the little gangsters are going to come creeping out of their hideouts to back him up; and if the head is a saint, then all the saints will suddenly appear and take their places by his side as though they all knew each other in advance.

Now you can see why the best, most desirable thing for a disciple is to install at the summit of his being the most marvellous head of all, that which the Cabbalah calls the White Head. When a disciple has reached the point of placing God at the summit of his being, he can be sure that Angels and Archangels will come with Him to keep him company. As the Lord cannot bear to be surrounded by demons, they are immediately evicted, and all of Heaven comes and sings in His presence — it could not be otherwise!

So this is true transformation, true alchemy, true magic: to install a new head. And in order to do so the least a disciple must do is to say, 'I don't want to be the one to give orders; I want to be a servant and obey and work. It is the Lord who must come and reign in me.' And, having said this he must work as hard as he can, because when the Lord sees that he has made everything ready and conditions are right, He will come, He will establish His dwelling place in the disciple. And wherever the Lord goes, the spirits of light go too, and settle all around. So, you see, just one change at the head, and all the rest is changed : it is inevitable. How could the Lord decide to go and settle somewhere and then find Himself alone or surrounded by demons ? It is inconceivable ! No, no ! God always travels in the company of a marvellously beautiful train of followers.

If only you took the trouble to understand the meaning and value of the hierarchy you would achieve fantastic results.

10

THE SYNARCHY WITHIN

Human beings are convinced that they hold objective and disinterested opinions about all the problems of life. They do not realize that, in point of fact, it is their inclinations and instinctive tendencies which determine those opinions. It begins when they are only children: when a child thinks that his mother is bad because she will not let him eat as many sweets and as much jam as he wants, he is convinced that his opinion is completely objective. And as the years go by and he reaches old age, even though his tastes and desires change, they continue to reflect his instinctive tendencies. In fact you could say that most ideologies or philosophical systems have grown out of human needs and inclinations and, often enough, unfortunately, out of their basest needs and inclinations.

Take the example of all the different theories about human sexuality: since most men and women are incapable of controlling their sexual energy, the specialists have invented all kinds of theories and rules which, in fact, have no absolute value. They only apply to weak, ignorant human beings who don't know (and who don't want to know) that instead of wasting their sexual energy in the quest for pleasure, they could be using it for a fantastic work. And the same holds true for all the other areas of life. This is why it is so difficult to instruct human beings: they can only accept and understand initiatic truths to the extent to which they have managed to free themselves from their basest needs, otherwise these needs continue to determine their mistaken opinions.

You could find other examples in political regimes: in Ancient Rome the populace had to be wooed with bread and circuses. And even now, although they may take other forms, people still clamour for bread and circuses. If anyone tries to suggest other goals and, especially, if he tries to get them to see that the form of government they have chosen reflects man's coarsest and most egotistical tendencies and that many things could be changed and improved, he is labelled as an enemy, a dangerous subversive who is plotting to disrupt the country and human society.

For centuries, the most common form of government was a monarchy. Was this normal?

Yes, certainly, because the universe is a monarchy, and God is the King who rules the whole of creation. It was perfectly natural, therefore, that the universal prototype should be reflected in miniature by human governments. But as very few monarchs were worthy of their task, monarchies were gradually overthrown and democracies took their place. And nowadays, democratic forms of government are generally preferred because they give their citizens greater opportunities for action and self-expression. Yes, as long as truly competent, enlightened and highly qualified people have not been found — by which I mean people who possess true Initiatic Science, who are capable of exercising an authentic authority with a complete lack of self-interest and who are willing to give their whole lives for the good of the human collectivity — then, yes, the democratic system is certainly the best.

In my lectures about Agharta[1] I talked to you about the *Synarchy*, which is the term used by Saint-Yves d'Alveydre in describing the form of government in that kingdom in the centre of the earth. At the head of this government there is a trinity, three persons, known as the Brahatma, the Mahatma and the Mahanga. The Brahatma represents Authority; the Mahatma, Power, and

1. See volume 25 of the 'Complete Works', chapter 8, part 5.

the Mahanga, the Executive. Below these three, reflecting the twelve signs of the Zodiac, is a group of twelve persons; and below them, another group of twenty-two who represent the twenty-two principles of the Word used by God in creating the universe and, finally, there is a group of three hundred and sixty-five persons, reflecting the three hundred and sixty-five days of the year.

The synarchic form of government, therefore, is in the image of the cosmic order established by God: God rules, the Archangels carry out His orders and the spirits of nature work throughout the universe to create and distribute its resources. This is the perfect order established by God, but instead of conforming to this order, human beings have invented all kinds of other arrangements more to their taste: and that is what anarchy is. You must not believe that anarchy is necessarily a total absence of order. Even if those who govern are unscrupulous, violent and avaricious and the wise have been eliminated, it is still a hierarchy, a hierarchy in reverse no doubt, but a hierarchy all the same. Even in anarchy there is someone at the top, someone who has taken the power into his own hands, and the others obey him because they know he is the strongest. But instead of choosing perfection and collective harmony as their goal, they choose disorder, that is to say the destruction of the divine order.

So a synarchy is the only form of government which truly manifests the hierarchy. However, there is one point which very few people, even those who are deeply spiritual, have understood and on which I want to insist so that you shall not misunderstand me, and that is that synarchy is, first and foremost, a form of hierarchy which must be established within each one of us. It is not possible to understand fully what synarchy really is if one has not understood the question of the Trinity. The Trinity of Father, Son and Holy Spirit is to be found in most major religions (Osiris, Isis and Horus in Ancient Egypt; Brahma, Vishnu and Shiva in Hinduism, and so on), and it exists within man in the form of power, love and wisdom.

Now let us look at the diagram on the following page.

The lower trinity, composed of the will, the heart and the mind, cannot solve any problems if it is not linked to the higher trinity of divine power, love and wisdom. When Hermes Trismegistus in his Emerald Tablet said, 'That which is below is like to that which is above, and that which is above is like to that which is below', he

THE HIGHER TRINITY

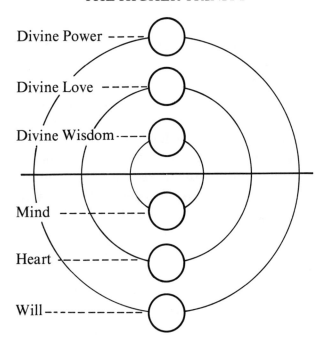

THE LOWER TRINITY

Figure 2.

did not specify exactly what form that correspondence took. But you have certainly walked by the edge of a lake and admired the reflection of houses and trees in the water, haven't you? And in this case you have seen that the reflection is always upside down. So that which is below, therefore, is like that which is on high, but reversed. And the surface of the water represents the frontier between the world above and the world below, a frontier below which people and things are no more than a reflection of reality. And this diagram illustrates this: that which is on the bottom of the lower level corresponds to that which is on top on the higher level, and so on.

When, through years of spiritual discipline and exercises, a disciple succeeds in attracting this higher Trinity into himself, it necessarily introduces the rule of synarchy into his whole being, and this is precisely what I want to be sure you understand, for it is essential: before a synarchical form of government can exist in the world it must exist within each and every human being. True synarchy is a state of affairs in which each individual gives absolute priority to the divine principle within him, thereby becoming capable of understanding, feeling and behaving according to the rules of divine law.

Once this is established, whether there are three persons at the head of a synarchical government or not, is not what matters most. The most important, in fact the only indispensable condition, is that there be at least one being who has developed the three higher principles within him-

self to the point of perfection. For it is these three
principles which have to govern together (the
word synarchy comes from the Greek *sun*, with,
and *archein*, to rule). Everybody could trust such
a being not to exploit or despoil them and it is this
trust and confidence which would make everything possible. For it is doubt, distrust and criti-
cism which destroy human beings: they need to
be able to trust and admire someone and follow
his leadership. That is why religion teaches people to put all their trust in the Lord and to love and
adore Him, so that they may be fulfilled and
reach eternal life.

But we have to go even further: Jesus said,
'Thy will be done on earth as it is in heaven', and
this means that Heaven must be present on earth.
The Lord above is not enough: He is so far away!
We need beings in every country who can
represent the Lord because they have established
the synarchy within themselves. For the moment
such beings are extremely rare, and when one or
other does appear, there are always some who
would rather get rid of them again as soon as possible: they find it very awkward to have people
near them who are so enlightened and capable of
seeing other people's crimes and weaknesses.

But you, at least, endeavour to accept the
synarchy and, first and foremost, to establish it
within yourselves. And since it is so difficult to

convince others, you would do better to leave them alone and get on with the business of becoming king in your own kingdom again. You must no longer accept to be the 'ex-king', deposed by your own subjects and cast into the deepest dungeon to survive on bread and water. This is the situation most human beings are in, and they don't even realize it: they still delude themselves that they are in charge! God created man in His own image and it is man who turned away from God. And now it is up to man to turn back again and reconquer his original dignity. This is the veritable meaning of synarchy.

Personally, I discovered this notion of synarchy when I was about seventeen. Of course, I did not call it that at the time, but I was profoundly struck by the fact that man's physical body only functions smoothly if all his organs obey a higher principle which governs their functions and unites them into one organism; that the physical dimension is related to a higher level, the dimension of feelings, and that feelings are, in turn, connected to an even higher dimension, that of thought, and so on, up the scale. And this is how I arrived at the spirit, the higher Self, that all-powerful, all-knowing principle which dwells at the peak point of our being, from where it organizes and governs the whole. Then my great concern was to learn how to communicate with this being and beg him to take possession of my inner kingdom, for he is the only one who is capable of governing it. After a great deal of searching I found that I could concentrate on a point on the back of my head, just at the base of the skull, and it was with this exercise that I got the best results.

If you want to establish the synarchy within yourself, you have to get in touch with your spirit, your higher Self, and persuade him to take over the direction of your whole being. If you do nothing to get in touch with him he will not intervene. Are you ill? In pain? Miserably unhappy? No matter! He will simply look on without being moved in any way, for he never suffers. But since it is man's vocation to attain the perfection of his own higher Self through a life of spiritual discipline and the application of suitable methods, he does have the possibility of getting in touch with him and, once he makes up his mind to do so, his higher Self can work wonders in him. But until man turns to him for help, his higher Self looks on stony-faced and untroubled by his antics or his suffering.

To work for the synarchy means to succeed in persuading your higher Self, your spirit, who is perfect, to take possession of your whole being, for then it is he, your true Self, who imposes his will in all circumstances. Instead of giving in to temptation all day long, and having to say, 'I couldn't help it', you will be able to say that it was you, yourself, who deliberately chose to do thus and so, and not some dark, unidentified force acting within you without your knowledge or consent. Then you will have found true freedom.

When we are all here, together, you have the best possible conditions for working with your higher Self. In contrast to what goes on in other schools, you do not come here to nourish your minds alone, but to renew and strengthen your bonds with Heaven, to experience spiritual emotions which will help you to discover new dimensions within yourselves. That is why, all together, we must immerse ourselves in a work in which the heart, the soul and the spirit have the most important role. The task of the intellect is to show us the best path to take and to point out all the reasons for taking that path: that is all. All the rest has to be done by the heart, the soul and the spirit. The intellect can only touch the surface, not the essence.

It is one thing to possess great intellectual possibilities; it is quite another to possess the light. Personally I have no talent and no intellectual capacity and I am hopelessly ignorant; but God has given me something else which is never appreciated: He has given me light, and it is the light that gives me the power to lead men toward the synarchy.

So always remember this: the true synarchy is when each one of us submits to the divine principle which dwells within him. As long as the synarchy does not reign in each individual, it cannot be established in the world, either.

By the same author:

Izvor Collection

201 - Toward a Solar Civilization

It is not enough to be familiar with the astronomical theory of heliocentricity. Since the sun is the centre of our universe, we must learn to put it at the centre of all our preoccupations and activities.

202 - Man, Master of His Destiny

If human beings are to be masters of their own destiny, they must understand that the laws which govern their physical, psychic and spiritual life are akin to those which govern the universe.

203 - Education Begins Before Birth

Humanity will improve and be transformed only when people realize the true import of the act of conception. In this respect, men and women have a tremendous responsibility for which they need years of preparation.

204 - The Yoga of Nutrition

The way we eat is as important as what we eat. Through our thoughts and feelings, it is possible to extract from our food spiritual elements which can contribute to the full flowering of our being.

205 - Sexual Force or the Winged Dragon

How to master, domesticate and give direction to our sexual energy so as to soar to the highest spheres of the spirit.

206 - A Philosophy of Universality

We must learn to replace our restricted, self-centred point of view with one that is immensely broad and universal. If we do this we shall all benefit; not only materially but particularly on the level of consciousness.

207 - What is a Spiritual Master

A true spiritual Master is, first, one who is conscious of the essential truths written by cosmic intelligence into the great book of Nature. Secondly, he must have achieved complete mastery of the elements of his own being. Finally, all the knowledge and authority he has acquired must serve only to manifest the qualities and virtues of selfless love.

208 - Under the Dove, the Reign of Peace

Peace will finally reign in the world only when human beings work to establish peace within themselves, in their every thought, feeling and action.

209 - Christmas and Easter in the Initiatic Tradition
Human beings are an integral part of the cosmos and intimately concerned by the process of gestation and birth going on in nature. Christmas and Easter – rebirth and resurrection – are simply two ways of envisaging humanity's regeneration and entry into the spiritual life.

210 - The Tree of the Knowledge of Good and Evil
Methods, not explanations, are the only valid answers to the problem of evil. Evil is an inner and outer reality which confronts us every day, and we must learn to deal with it.

211 - Freedom, the Spirit Triumphant
A human being is a spirit, a spark sprung from within the Almighty. Once a person understands, sees and feels this truth, he will be free.

212 - Light is a Living Spirit
Light, the living matter of the universe, is protection, nourishment and an agency for knowledge for human beings. Above all, it is the only truly effective means of self-transformation.

213 - Man's Two Natures, Human and Divine
Man is that ambiguous creature that evolution has placed on the borderline between the animal world and the divine world. His nature is ambivalent, and it is this ambivalence that he must understand and overcome.

214 - Hope for the World: Spiritual Galvanoplasty
On every level of the universe, the masculine and feminine principles reproduce the activity of those two great cosmic principles known as the Heavenly Father and the Divine Mother of which every manifestation of nature and life are a reflection. Spiritual galvanoplasty is a way of applying the science of these two fundamental principles to one's inner life.

215 - The True Meaning of Christ's Teaching
Jesus incorporated into the Our Father – or Lord's Prayer – an ancient body of knowledge handed down by Tradition and which had existed long before his time. A vast universe is revealed to one who knows how to interpret each of the requests formulated in this prayer.

216 - The Living Book of Nature
Everything in nature is alive and it is up to us to learn how to establish a conscious relationship with creation so as to receive that life within ourselves.

217 - New Light on the Gospels
The Parables and other tales from the Gospels are here interpreted as situations and events applicable to our own inner life.

218 - The Symbolic Language of Geometrical Figures

Each geometrical figure – circle, triangle, pentagram, pyramid or cross – is seen as a structure fundamental to the organization of the macrocosm (the universe) and the microcosm (human beings).

219 - Man's Subtle Bodies and Centres

However highly developed our sense organs, their scope will never reach beyond the physical plane. To experience richer and subtler sensations, human beings must exercise the subtler organs and spiritual centres that they also possess: the aura, the solar plexus, the Hara centre, the Chakras, and so on.

220 - The Zodiac, Key to Man and to the Universe

Those who are conscious of being part of the universe feel the need to work inwardly in order to find within themselves the fullness of the cosmic order so perfectly symbolized by the Zodiac.

221 - True Alchemy or The Quest for Perfection

Instead of fighting our weaknesses and vices – we would inevitably be defeated – we must learn to make them work for us. We think it normal to harness the untamed forces of nature, so why be surprised when a Master, an initiate, speaks of harnessing the primitive forces within us? This is true spiritual alchemy.

222 - Man's Psychic Life: Elements and Structures

"Know thyself" How to interpret this precept carved over the entrance to the temple at Delphi? To know oneself is to be conscious of one's different bodies, from the denser to the most subtle, of the principles which animate these bodies, of the needs they induce in one, and of the state of consciousness which corresponds to each.

223 - Creation: Artistic and Spiritual

Everyone needs to create but true creation involves spiritual elements. Artists, like those who seek the spirit, have to reach beyond themselves in order to receive elements from the higher planes.

224 - The Powers of Thought

Thought is a power, an instrument given to us by God so that we may become creators like himself – creators in beauty and perfection. This means that we must be extremely watchful, constantly verifying that what we do with our thoughts is truly for our own good and that of the whole world. This is the one thing that matters.

225 -Harmony and Health

Illness is a result of some physical or psychic disorder. The best defence against illness, therefore, is harmony. Day and night we must take care to be attuned and in harmony with life as a whole, with the boundless life of the cosmos.

226 - The Book of Divine Magic

True, divine magic, consists in never using the faculties, knowledge, or powers one has acquired for one's own self-interest, but always and only for the establishment of God's kingdom on earth.

227 - Golden Rules for Everyday Life

Why spoil one's life by chasing after things that matter less than life itself? Those who learn to give priority to life, who protect and preserve it in all integrity, will find more and more that they obtain their desires. For it is this, an enlightened, luminous life that can give them everything.

228 - Looking into the Invisible

Meditation, dreams, visions, astral projection all give us access to the invisible world, but the quality of the revelations received depends on our efforts to elevate and refine our perceptions.

229 - The Path of Silence

In every spiritual teaching, practices such as meditation and prayer have only one purpose: to lessen the importance attributed to one's lower nature and give one's divine nature more and more scope for expression. Only in this way can a human being experience true silence.

230 - The Book of Revelations: A Commentary

If *Revelations* is a difficult book to interpret it is because we try to identify the people, places and events it describes instead of concentrating on the essence of its message: a description of the elements and processes of our spiritual life in relation to the life of the cosmos.

231 - The Seeds of Happiness

Happiness is like a talent which has to be cultivated. Those who want to possess happiness must go in search of the elements which will enable them to nourish it inwardly; elements which belong to the divine world.

232 - The Mysteries of Fire and Water

Our psychic life is fashioned every day by the forces we allow to enter us, the influences that impregnate us. What could be more poetic, more meaningful than water and fire and the different forms under which they appear?

233 - Youth: Creators of the Future
Youth is full of life, enthusiasms and aspirations of every kind. The great question is how to channel its extraordinary, overflowing effervescence of energies.

234 - Truth, Fruit of Wisdom and Love
We all abide by our own "truth", and it is in the name of their personal "truth" that human beings are continually in conflict. Only those who possess true love and true wisdom discover the same truth and speak the same language.

235 - In Spirit and in Truth
Since we live on earth we are obliged to give material form to our religious beliefs. Sacred places and objects, rites, prayers and ceremonies are expressions of those beliefs. It is important to understand that they are no more than expressions – expressions which are always more or less inadequate. They are not themselves the religion, for religion exists in spirit and in truth.

236 - Angels and Other Mysteries of the Tree of Life
God is like a pure current of electricity which can reach us only through a series of transformers. These transformers are the countless luminous beings which inhabit the heavens and which tradition calls the Angelic Hierarchies. It is through them that we receive divine life; through them that we are in contact with God.

237 - Cosmic Balance, the Secret of Polarity
Libra – the Scales – symbolizes cosmic balance, the equilibrium of the two opposite and complementary forces, the masculine and feminine principles, by means of which the universe came into being and continues to exist. The symbolism of Libra, expression of this twofold polarity, dominates the whole of creation.

By the same author
(translated from the French)

"Complete Works" Collection

Volume	1 —	The Second Birth
Volume	2 —	Spiritual Alchemy
Volume	5 —	Life Force
Volume	6 —	Harmony
Volume	7 —	The Mysteries of Yesod
Volume	10 —	The Splendour of Tiphareth
		The Yoga of the Sun
Volume	11 —	The Key to the Problems of Existence
Volume	12 —	Cosmic Moral Law
Volume	13 —	A New Earth
		Methods, Exercises, Formulas, Prayers
Volume	14 —	Love and Sexuality (Part I)
Volume	15 —	Love and Sexuality (Part II)
Volume	17 —	'Know Thyself' Jnana Yoga (Part I)
Volume	18 —	'Know Thyself' Jnana Yoga (Part II)
Volume	25 —	A New Dawn: Society and Politics in the Light of Initiatic Science (Part I)
Volume	26 —	A New Dawn: Society and Politics in the Light of Initiatic Science (Part II)
Volume	29 —	On the Art of Teaching (Part III)
Volume	30 —	Life and Work in an Initiatic School
		Training for the Divine
Volume	32 —	The Fruits of the Tree of Life
		The Cabbalistic Tradition

Brochures:

New Presentation

301 —	The New Year
302 —	Meditation
303 —	Respiration
304 —	Death and the Life Beyond

Live Recordings on Tape

KC2510An — The Laws of Reincarnation
(Two audio cassettes)

(available in French only)

K 2001 Fr — La science de l'unité
K 2002 Fr — Le bonheur
K 2003 Fr — La vraie beauté
K 2004 Fr — L'éternel printemps
K 2005 Fr — La loi de l'enregistrement
K 2006 Fr — La science de l'éducation
K 2007 Fr — La prière
K 2008 Fr — L'esprit et la matière
K 2009 Fr — Le monde des archétypes
K 2010 Fr — L'importance de l'ambiance
K 2011 Fr — Le yoga de la nutrition
K 2012 Fr — L'aura
K 2013 Fr — Déterminisme et indéterminisme
K 2014 Fr — Les deux natures de l'être humain
K 2015 Fr — Prendre et donner
K 2016 Fr — La véritable vie spirituelle
K 2017 Fr — La mission de l'art
K 2018 Fr — Il faut laisser l'amour véritable se manifester
K 2019 Fr — Comment orienter la force sexuelle
K 2020 Fr — Un haut idéal pour la jeunesse
K 2021 Fr — La réincarnation - Preuves de la réincarnation
dans les Évangiles.
K 2022 Fr — La réincarnation - Rien ne se produit par hasard,
une intelligence préside à tout.
K 2023 Fr — La réincarnation - L'aura et la réincarnation.
K 2024 Fr — La loi de la responsabilité
K 2551 Fr — La réincarnation (coffret de 3 cassettes)
K 2552 Fr — Introduction à l'astrologie initiatique
(coffret de 3 cassettes)
K 2553 Fr — La méditation (coffret de 3 cassettes)

World Wide - Editor-Distributor
Editions PROSVETA S.A. - B.P. 12 - F - 83601 Fréjus Cedex (France)
Tel. (00 33) 04 94 40 82 41 - Fax (00 33) 04 94 40 80 05
Web: **www.prosveta.com**
E-mail: **international@prosveta.com**

Distributors

AUSTRALIA
SURYOMA LTD
P.O. Box 798 – Brookvale – N.S.W. 2100
Tel. / Fax: (61) 2 9984 8500 – E-mail: suryoma@csi.com

AUSTRIA
HARMONIEQUELL VERSAND – A-5302 Henndorf, Hof 37
Tel. / Fax: (43) 6214 7413 – E-mail: info@prosveta.at

BELGIUM
PROSVETA BENELUX – Liersesteenweg 154 B-2547 Lint
Tel.: (32) 3/455 41 75 – Fax: 3/454 24 25
N.V. MAKLU Somersstraat 13-15 – B-2000 Antwerpen
Tel.: (32) 3/321 29 00 – E-mail: prosveta@skynet.be
VANDER S.A. – Av. des Volontaires 321 – B-1150 Bruxelles
Tel.: (32) 27 62 98 04 – Fax: 27 62 06 62

BRAZIL
NOBEL SA – Rua da Balsa, 559 – CEP 02910 - São Paulo, SP

BULGARIA
SVETOGLED – Bd Saborny 16 A, appt 11 – 9000 Varna
E-mail: svetgled@revolta.com

CANADA
PROSVETA Inc. – 3950, Albert Mines – North Hatley, QC J0B 2C0
Tel.: (1) 819 564-8212 – Fax: (1) 819 564-1823
In Canada, call toll free: 1-800-854-8212
E-mail: prosveta@prosveta-canada.com — www.prosveta-canada.com

COLUMBIA
PROSVETA – Avenida 46 no 19-14 (Palermo) – Santafé de Bogotá
Tel.: (57) 232-01-36 – Fax: (57) 633-58-03

CYPRUS
THE SOLAR CIVILISATION BOOKSHOP
73 D Kallipoleos Avenue - Lycavitos – P.O. Box 4947, 1355 – Nicosia
Tel.: 02 377503 and 09 680854

CZECH REPUBLIC
PROSVETA Tchèque – Ant. Sovy 18 – České Budejovice 370 05
Tel. / Fax: 0042038-53 00 227 – E-mail: prosveta@seznam.cz

GERMANY
PROSVETA Deutschland – Postfach 16 52 – 78616 Rottweil
Tel.: (49) 741 46551 – Fax: (49) 741 46552 – E-mail: Prosveta.de@t-online.de
EDIS GmbH, Mühlweg 2 – 82054 Sauerlach
Tel.: (49) 8104-6677-0 – Fax: (49) 8104-6677-99

GREAT BRITAIN & IRELAND
PROSVETA – The Doves Nest, Duddleswell Uckfield – East Sussex TN 22 3JJ
Tel.: (44) (01825) 712988 – Fax: (44) (01825) 713386
E-mail: prosveta@pavilion.co.uk

GREECE
PROSVETA – VAMVACAS INDUSTRIAL EQUIPEMENT
Moutsopoulou 103 – 18541 Piraeus
HAITI
B.P. 115 – Jacmel, Haiti (W.I .) – Tel. / Fax: (509) 288-3319
HOLLAND
STICHTING PROSVETA NEDERLAND
Zeestraat 50 – 2042 LC Zandvoort – E-mail: prosveta@worldonline.nl
HONG KONG
SWINDON BOOK CO LTD
246 Deck 2, Ocean Terminal – Harbour City – Tsimshatsui, Kowloon
ISRAEL
ÉDITIONS GALATAIA – 58 Bar-Kohva street – Tel Aviv
Tel.: 00 972 3 5286264 – Fax: 00 972 3 5286260
ITALY
PROSVETA Coop. – Casella Postale – 06060 Moiano (PG)
Tel. / Fax: (39) 075-8358498 – E-mail: prosveta@tin.it
LUXEMBOURG
PROSVETA BENELUX – Liersesteenweg 154 - B-2547 Lint
NORWAY
PROSVETA NORDEN – Postboks 5101 – 1503 Moss
Tel.: 69 26 51 40 – Fax: 69 25 06 76
E-mail: prosveta Norden – prosnor@online.no
PORTUGAL
PUBLICAÇÕES EUROPA-AMERICA Ltd
Est Lisboa-Sintra KM 14 – 2726 Mem Martins Codex
ROMANIA
ANTAR – Str. N. Constantinescu 10 – Bloc 16A - sc A - Apt. 9
Sector 1 – 71253 Bucarest
Tel.: (40) 1 679 52 48 – Tel. / Fax: (40) 1 231 37 19
RUSSIA
Neapolitensky – 40 Gorohovaya - Appt 1 – Saint-Petersbourg
Tel.: (70) 812 5327 184 / (70) 812 2726 876 – Fax: (70) 812 1582 363
SINGAPORE & MALAYSIA
AMERICASIA GLOBAL MARKETING – Clementi Central Post Office
P.O. Box 108 – Singapore 911204 – Tel.: (65) 892 0503 – Fax: (65) 95 199 198
E-mail: harvard1@mbox4.singnet.com.sg
SPAIN
ASOCIACIÓN PROSVETA ESPAÑOLA – C/ Ausias March n° 23 Ático
SP-08010 Barcelona — Tel.: (34) (3) 412 31 85 – Fax: (34) (3) 302 13 72
SWITZERLAND
PROSVETA Société Coopérative – CH - 1808 Les Monts-de-Corsier
Tel.: (41) 21 921 92 18 – Fax: (41) 21 922 92 04
E-mail: prosveta@swissonline.ch
UNITED STATES
PROSVETA U.S.A. – P.O. Box 1176 – New Smyrna Beach, FL.32170-1176
Tel. / Fax: (904) 428-1465
E-mail: sales@prosveta-usa .com — www.prosveta-usa.com
VENEZUELA
BETTY MUNÕZ – Urbanización Los Corales – avenida Principal
Quinta La Guarapa – LA GUAÏRA – Municipio Vargas

Printed by
Imprimerie H.L.N.
Sherbrooke (Quebec) Canada
in March 2000